HOMERUN LEADERSHIP

Your Guide to **Better, Faster** Team Decisions

Dr. Dave Webb

HOMERUN LEADERSHIP
Your Guide to Better, Faster Team Decisions

Copyright © 2022 by Dr. Dave Webb

Printed in the United States of America

Designed by Ivan Stojić

First Printing: 2022

I dedicate this book to my wife Julie,
who has been my everything for our 28 years together.
Love, Dave

Acknowledgements

It's difficult to know where to begin to thank all the people who made it possible for me to complete this book. There are many!

I'm first of all thankful for great parents. My mom and dad always modeled that the key to success was more education. After I earned my doctorate, my mom always said that I was the only person she knew who actually used their dissertation daily. I finished writing my dissertation 20 years ago, and I have continued practicing what I studied. My dream has been to write a user-friendly version of all the challenging science in my research. When my parents passed away a few years ago, I committed to achieving the goal of writing a book to simplify the best leadership science of four. This book now distills the most essential leadership learnings down to a simplified science to help leaders increase their success every day. Thanks, mom and dad!

My family has been my greatest encouragement and support to help see this project to completion. My wife Julie, an 18-year cancer survivor, has always been my greatest support. My kids, Benjamin, Anna, Megan, and Sarah, all provided incredible feedback and encouragement along this lengthy journey. My brother Tom has been an outstanding editor on each revision. My brother Bill has provided me outstanding daily guidance and support, mixed with many lousy jokes. And my whole extended family has provided support and feedback throughout this writing process. Many of them have used IROD and have much to show in return.

Thank you to Kevin Johnson, my book coach, who helped me finalize years of ideas and iterations into a succinct guide to better, faster team decisions. And thanks to Jane Kise for introducing me to Kevin so I could get this book done! I also thank Richard Dodson for serving as my chief editor and book producer to see this book to completion.

The greatest learnings that enabled me to write both my dissertation and this book were provided by some amazing teachers:

- Dr. Mirja Hanson taught me the most about facilitation and the importance of asking great questions to guide your team to success. Her ToP training was influential in helping me see the science of four.
- Diane Gossen taught me restorative practices, and her restorative science of four steps have helped me to repair more relationships over the past 20 years than any other framework.
- John Conbere taught me critical skills and components of mediation, and the critical four key steps that are crucial to the success of resolving team disagreements.
- Dr. Chad Schmidt taught me about the four preferences in group work thanks to the National School Reform Faculty. Thanks also to the National School Reform Faculty for their permission to create my adaptations to their framework. Their four types overlaid on all of the other sciences of four and help to further explain how our team type impacts team decision-making.
- I had so many starts and stops along my 20-year journey to write this user-friendly version of my dissertation. Thank you to Karlyn Lind, Nicholas Erickson, Darcy Schatz, and Lisa Brandecker for your help and support, encouragement, and writing assistance along this journey.

Finally, I thank the many former colleagues over the years. Your support and leadership, and willingness to partner as a team has helped us serve families well. You have brought me great joy and inspiration.

Table of Contents

CHAPTER 1

Why Homerun Leadership?

Two roads diverged in a wood, and I—
I took the one less traveled by,
And that has made all the difference.

ROBERT FROST

This book is for new leaders. And in today's world, we're all new leaders. The shift from employee to manager, from manager to executive, from teacher to administrator, from staff member to pastor, from adult to parent, from single to couple, are incredibly challenging. As a leader, moving your team from point A to point B can feel overwhelming. But the path of good leadership, sound decision-making, and real change is predictable—and attainable.

Pause for a moment and envision your next leadership meeting. How would you feel if you knew—ahead of time—the questions your team would ask? Or if—before you sit down to meet with your team—you could easily identify the steps you need to complete to be fully prepared?

Homerun Leadership gave me that gift.

With the average tenure of superintendents in America being just a few years, I credit the process in this book for helping me successfully complete a dozen years as a high school principal and a dozen more as a superintendent of schools.

Homerun Leadership gives me the answers ahead of time and will for you, too.

The formula I call "IROD" distills years of research into an easy-to-understand, memorable, repeatable process that helps you and your team make great decisions. It's the Homerun Leadership System.

Knowing the core science of 4 that drives all change and decision-making has given me the confidence to do the difficult job of leadership. It also allows me to teach, coach, and mentor others on this most critical leadership skill.

Homerun Leadership drives you forward by giving you a framework applicable to ANY situation and EVERY meeting. When you know the questions your team will ask—and want answered—you're ready to lead.

For me, IROD is "The Road Always Traveled." Not because team leaders intentionally go down this path. They usually don't. Especially when things get heated. But it's the road all leaders eventually travel when they truly want their team to move forward. We know the realities behind IROD intuitively. Smart leaders see the benefit of this intentional science-based winning leadership formula.

When team leaders deviate from the formula, they veer into trouble. It's inevitable. But Homerun Leadership makes a proven method for success accessible to everyone.

If you follow the IROD process (the decision-making science of **Information, Reactions, Options, Decision**), you will act on what research says about how people naturally make decisions. You will implement the wisdom of all the major change-management systems. And you will be inclusive of all the voices on your team.

If you stay on this path to get from point A to point B, you will notice decreasing team resistance and team stress. Moreover, as you rack up team wins, you will build positive momentum and help increase success for the entire organization.

That's what I call a Homerun!

For bonus video clips, go to **HomerunLeadership.com/Bonus**

CHAPTER 2

Regular Leader, Regular Leadership

Do the best you can until you know better.
Then when you know better, do better.

MAYA ANGELOU

A guy I know well was just 29 when he landed his dream job directing a premier language-learning camp serving hundreds of children and youth each summer. He had worked at the northern Minnesota camp for years, in many different roles, climbing the organizational ladder summer after summer.

This guy had watched some previous directors do well. He had seen several other leaders struggle, including some who crashed and burned spectacularly. He had yearned for the day he would take charge and set direction.

He was beyond excited to get his shot as top leader.

He felt confident his leadership would be different. He was ready. Or so he thought.

On a warm early July day, exactly a week before the kids showed up, staff arrived.

Staff orientation was a disaster. By the end of the first week with campers, four counselors had quit, leaving the team shorthanded, further increasing everyone's stress, and making the month until new staff could be hired incredibly difficult.

It was an obvious sign of the new camp director's ineffective leadership.

Ineffective? His leadership style was worse than that. It was unintentionally hurting programs and staff.

When something needed doing, the director didn't engage team members in planning and decision-making. He just told them to get it done. He repeatedly deployed his signature skill of giving directives, sometimes with a dose of Minnesota Nice. Sometimes not-so-nice. But always telling people what to do. Over and over. He was certain he could rely on his own wisdom and intuition to make decisions on behalf of himself, staff, and campers.

The rookie camp director had never learned a better way to lead. He was a Regular Leader doing Regular Leadership.

The camp director lacked a critical component of leadership: knowing how to partner with his team and lead them in making great decisions. While he was bursting with good intentions, he had no skills or techniques to use once in the role.

By the end of summer, this guy was exhausted, demoralized, and totally relieved to get back to his teaching job, where he alone made the rules and could simply tell the kids what to do.

As you might suspect, I know that guy all too well. He's me. I was a Regular Leader who only knew Regular Leadership.

Now I Know

When I started in my camp director role, I attempted to replicate what I perceived as the best of leaders who had come before me. I had good intentions, but I lacked skills. I didn't grasp the basics of team dynamics. And I clearly didn't know how to lead. My leadership style was random. Reactive. A mess. I couldn't understand why it was so maddening and so stressful.

And I didn't know anything about **IROD**, the decision-making core leadership science of four—**Information, Reactions, Options, Decision.**

Those four process points are the secret to the kind of team-based decisions that move organizations forward.

Maya Angelou says, "Do the best you can until you know better. Then when you know better, do better." I did the best I could, not realizing there was a better way to lead.

I wish I had known how to better:

- Support my teammates.
- Harness their talents.
- Pull together to reach a common goal.

Maximizing the best gifts of the team to make the best team decisions is the key skill of leaders. That skill makes possible amazing new plans, team-supported agreements, consistent follow-through, and the best possible results.

I wish I knew this when I started as a leader.

Now I know.

And success has everything to do with IROD. There's a science of leadership success, and IROD is the winning leadership formula:

- There are four Homerun Leadership Types.
- Each Homerun Leadership Type favors one aspect of IROD, be it Information, Reactions, Options, or Decision.
- Each of the four Homerun Leadership Types has different needs that drive how they approach decisions.
- To satisfy these needs, a leader must ask four IROD questions.
- Asking these four Homerun questions in a specific order creates a repeatable process. It's the Homerun Basepath—the research-based four-step framework for reaching decisions.
- IROD, the core leadership science of four, is the key to all effective change, decision-making, and problem-solving systems.

The four Homerun Leadership Types match the four decision-making steps, which match the four IROD questions. This overlapping science increases the power of users to lead effectively because you only need to know four simple steps to maximize your success and positive team impact.

Now that I know better, I have been doing better by gradually shifting from Regular Leadership to Homerun Leadership. I still strike out, especially if I skip bases when I forget to use the process. But more and more, especially when I slow down and follow the base path, I can increase my success average, or "Leadership Batting Average."

Now I know IROD is the winning leadership formula for leadership success, as long as we learn to ask simple IROD questions.

Now I know my own calling is to help you to dramatically increase your success and the success of your team.

	IROD Chapter Review Questions
I	What are your key takeaways from this chapter?
R	What reactions do you have to the information shared in this chapter?
O	How did this chapter's ideas offer ways to enhance your decision-making process?
D	What ideas from this chapter could you apply immediately to your team's decision-making?

For bonus video clips, go to **HomerunLeadership.com/Bonus**

CHAPTER 3

IROD: The Core Leadership Science of Four

None of us is as smart as all of us.

RUDY PERPICH, former Governor of Minnesota

As a leader, you make decisions. It's what you do. The WHAT of those choices, however, is only half of the issue. HOW you undertake the process of decision-making determines whether:

- Your team breaks apart—or pulls together.
- Your organization moves backward—or forward.
- Your customers, clients, and other stakeholders abandon you—or join you for the bright future you.
- Your goals fail—or succeed.

The core of great leadership is repeatable success in decision-making. Great leadership is a compilation of your great decisions.

That's the challenge. How can you make outstanding decisions again and again?

Some of the best leadership practices I've gained from life, work, and schooling can be boiled down to simple but powerful ideas I call Homerun Leadership.

I'm not a baseball fanatic, but I've watched enough to understand a few facts:

- Baseball uses deliberate strategies—and a little luck—that come together in electrifying plays that change outcomes.
- Baseball offers a variety of ways to fail at bat—and miss your opportunity to score.
- Baseball demands you run the same bases in the same order—every time—or else.
- Baseball requires you get on base—but the only thing that really counts is getting as many players as possible around the basepath to home plate.

While base-clearing grand slams are spectacular, most ball games are won by a steady stream of hits—singles and doubles that put batters on base and move them around the diamond to home plate. In the context of leadership, that's how homeruns happen and teams win together.

My formal study and ongoing observations in diverse organizations tells me that leaders often fail at the core job of leading the decision-making process. They strike out. Frequently. Everywhere. All the time. Needlessly. Teams fail to score because leaders don't know how to move people around the bases. Most leaders don't know the bases exist, or how to run the bases to increase their team's success.

What I call "Regular Leadership" is the problem. We see it all around us. It's often unsuccessful in making decisions and moving people forward.

With Homerun Leadership, it's a whole new ballgame.

This book will teach you a repeatable process that moves people around the bases in your business, nonprofit, school, faith community, family, wherever. No matter your goals or the decisions you need to lead, you can use these steps to maximize your success. Everyone gets across home plate. Everyone scores. Everyone wins.

Homerun Leadership uses a baseball diamond framework to demonstrate multiple, overlapping leadership systems, all based on science. It's so easy to learn its basics that even before we get to the main part of this book, I'm going to give you three quick hits that introduce you to Homerun Leadership decisions:

Hit 1: Discover the Homerun Basepath—the research-based four-step process for reaching decisions.

Hit 2: Discover the Four Homerun Questions—specific questions in a specific order you ask to facilitate successful discussions and decisions.

Hit 3: Discover Your Own Homerun Team Leadership Type—your preferred approach to making decisions.

I promise to make this quick, and I'm confident you'll see how these discoveries will enhance your leadership.

Why Does This Matter?

Observationally, I believe Regular Leaders struggle much more than they succeed when leading team decisions.

Translation:

Rarely are leaders, their teams, their constituency, or other stakeholders satisfied with the results of decisions. Homerun Leadership empowers you to do far better.

All of us want to do better. Wouldn't it be great to get more leadership wins with less pain in the process?

More wins, less pain. That's my hope for you.

My goal with Homerun Leadership is to help you raise your "Leadership Batting Average" (LBA).

When you understand and relentlessly implement this methodology, you will struggle less and score more. While you can't control what circumstances throw at you, you can learn to respond more effectively.

Hit 1: Discover the Homerun Leadeship Basepath

In my role as a school superintendent, I train new board members almost every year. I recently gave two new board members a brief Homerun Leadership overview to ground them in how we make great team decisions. As I began, I said, "I'm going to share my best stuff with you today." One of my board members asked, "As opposed to what?"

Good question. But here's my reasoning. Whenever I attend a workshop or training session, I want to increase my leadership toolkit, taking away something new I can use immediately.

So here it is. Let me tell you about IROD, the basis of Homerun Leadership Types and the secret to awesome team decisions using the Homerun Leadership Basepath (Conbere, 1996; Spencer, 1989; Stanfield, 1997; "Technology of Participation," n.d.).

Let's start with this summary:

IROD – HOMERUN LEADERSHIP TYPES	
DESCRIPTIVE NAME	**SHORTHAND NAME**
INFORMATION	**1st** Baser
REACTIONS	**2nd** Baser
OPTIONS	**3rd** Baser
DECISION	**4th** Baser

You can identify each Homerun Leadership Type in two ways. The first is a descriptor, where the initial letter of each gives us IROD. The second is a shorthand name based on a ball diamond: 1st, 2nd, 3rd, or 4th Baser.

The real power of Homerun Leadership is understanding what each "baser" is looking for in a decision-making process. Each has a distinct priority, meaning they value asking and answering one of the following four points:

Information: Do we have all the INFORMATION on this topic?

Reactions: Do we have everyone's REACTIONS to the information?

Options: Have we brainstormed all the OPTIONS, listed pros and cons of each, and prioritized the list?

Decision: Is the DECISION the will of the group?

You can quickly increase your leadership success—your Leadership Batting Average (LBA)—by knowing IROD—with its four Homerun Leadership Types—and "running the bases" in order. This Homerun Basepath will get you asking all the right questions to bring you and your team markedly increased success.

IROD – THE HOMERUN LEADERSHIP BASEPATH				
	INFORMATION **1st Base**	**REACTIONS** **2nd Base**	**OPTIONS** **3rd Base**	**DECISIONS** **4th Base**
Homerun Base Running Task	Team members take time to ask questions to gather all the facts, data, details, and information regarding the issue or upcoming decision.	Team members take time to gather all the reactions, reflections, feedback, and concerns regarding the issue or upcoming decision.	Team members take time to gather and list all the options, ideas, possibilities, and choices. Team members also list all the pros and cons to each of the brainstormed options and prioritize the list of options.	Team members take time to eliminate less viable options to eventually select and agree (majority—the will of the group) to the best remaining option.
Homerun Base Cleanup Task	Before moving forward, team members double-check to make sure they have gathered all the information.	Before moving forward, team members double-check to make sure they have gathered all the reactions.	Before moving forward, team members double-check to make sure they have gathered all the options and prioritized the list.	Before reaching agreement, team members double-check to make sure they are moving with the will of the group.

Hit 2: Discover the Four Homerun Questions

Now for the next step in the basics of Homerun Leadership Decisions (Conbere, 1996; Spencer, 1989; Stanfield, 1997; "Technology of Participation," n.d.). Once you know the Homerun Basepath, I want you to begin using my best, simplified Homerun Questions. They're how you run the bases every time!

HOMERUN QUESTIONS (IROD)			
INITIAL	**BASE**	**QUESTION**	**CLEANUP QUESTION**
I	1st	Do we have all the INFORMATION on this topic?	Anything else?
R	2nd	Do we have everyone's REACTIONS to the information?	Anything else?
O	3rd	Have we brainstormed all the OPTIONS, listed pros and cons of each, and prioritized the list?	Anything else?
D	4th	Is the DECISION the will of the group?	Anything else?

Those Homerun questions (IROD) asked in order, in each decision-making situation, ensure you run the bases every time. The outcome? You score! Every person involved in the decision feels heard, and together you reach a well-reasoned choice respectful of the priorities of everyone involved.

As you picture using this process, don't miss the all-important Cleanup question for each base: "Anything else?" As you ask and answer each of the four IROD Homerun questions, this follow-up question ensures you complete that step. You know you're done when your team members offer no additional input.

Hit 3: Discover Your Homerun Team Leadership Type

The third step is to learn your own Homerun Team Leadership Type ("School Reform Initiative," 2017; Spencer, 1989; Stanfield, 1997). This type or preference affects your decision-making in team situations. Once you master your own type, you'll not only understand your own decision-making priority but see it in a larger context. You'll recognize how crucial all four Homerun Team Leadership Types are to managing good process and team decision-making in the people around you.

You'll also find you begin to place greater value on the gifts other people bring to your team—in particular, their approach to decision-making. They see things from a different vantage point, and that's incredibly valuable!

Chances are good you have teammates who frustrate you. As Homerun Leadership principles help you understand their approach to decision-making, your appreciation for other types will increase. You'll discover your own gaps and blind spots. I did.

In the end, you'll know exactly what each person on your team needs to feel good about your team decisions. In addition, your team will benefit from the best perspectives and input from each team member.

You can discover your Homerun Team Leadership Type using a quiz with just four questions. What are the four Homerun Team Leadership Types— and what is your type? Let's find out.

The Homerun Leadership Type Quiz

Your Homerun Team Leadership Type is your instinctive approach that most commonly comes out when you're in a decision-making situation. When your team is in a decision-making situation, it's how you show up.

LEADERSHIP TYPE	SIGNS OF YOUR LEADERSHIP TYPE	That's me! (checkmark)
1st BASER	*You may be a 1st Baser if:* When making decisions, you need to know **the detailed facts, data, and information**. You like to know the who, what, when, where, and why before acting.	
2nd BASER	*You may be a 2nd Baser if:* When making decisions, you need to know everyone's **feelings, feedback, reactions, and reflections** have been considered and that all voices are heard.	
3rd BASER	*You may be a 3rd Baser if:* When making decisions, you need to look at **the big picture** and brainstorm **all the possibilities, ideas, and options** to determine the best choice before acting.	
4th BASER	*You may be a 4th Baser if:* When making decisions, you need to act, try things, and jump in, and you thrive on **reaching a decision, agreement, plan, or recommendation**.	

Later in the book, I'll offer a more robust research-based Leadership Types Assessment you can use on your own and with your team. For now, where do you see yourself in those descriptions? Put a checkmark indicating your likely Leadership Type.

Your Leadership Type:

◆ Drives your *motivations* and *behavior*.

- Makes you *feel* good about a decision.
- Makes you *think* a decision is correct.

Your Leadership Type is what you care about most in a decision-making situation.

Everyone has a Homerun Leadership Type. Each of us brings

our gifts
our focus
our priorities
our emphasis
our interests
our behavior
our way of processing

to every meeting we attend.

Whatever your Homerun Leadership Type, it's critical you learn and understand the strengths and weakness areas of all four Leadership Types. That mastery will enable you to work effectively with each team member to meet their needs and reach successful, shared team decisions.

After all, nobody wants to live through a decision that brings heavy resistance from their team, and that's exactly what you get if you skip over the needs of your teammates' Leadership Type. Then, get ready for the OVERTHROW!

Here's the all-important application: In your leadership setting, it's critically important for a team to fully support the needs of all four Homerun Leadership Types. When you fully complete the tasks for each type, you make the best team decision.

Up Next

Got it? The THREE QUICK HITS introduce you to the best problem-solving and decision-making process for immediately increasing your success rate—your Leadership Batting Average.

Read on to learn why Homerun Leadership works—and how you can use it to lead through everyday issues as well as the more complicated circumstances you'll face as a leader.

	IROD Chapter Review Questions
I	What are your key takeaways from this chapter?
R	What reactions do you have to the information shared in this chapter?
O	How did this chapter's ideas offer ways to enhance your decision-making process?
D	What ideas from this chapter could you apply immediately to your team's decision-making?

For bonus video clips, go to **HomerunLeadership.com/Bonus**

CHAPTER 4

The Proven Four-Step Pattern

Systems thinking is a discipline for seeing wholes. It is a framework for seeing interrelationships rather than things, for seeing "patterns of change" rather than static "snapshots."

PETER SENGE—The Fifth Discipline

THREE YEARS after my stumbling first summer as camp director, I resigned and started a doctoral program in Educational Leadership. Early in that five-year journey, the high school where I taught Spanish experienced major conflict among the staff. Outside mediation trainers arrived and trained staff in resolving interpersonal conflict, teaching us **a four-step pattern** to reach a solution (Conbere, 1996). I was impressed at the power of four simple questions to reach a resolution by hearing each participant's story and concerns, followed by collaboratively brainstorming possible solutions. When structured correctly, these four steps drive conflict management results that support the needs of each participant.

Not much later, a classmate invited me to attend a "Technology of Partic-ipation" training session she was leading, which gave me an opportunity to gain experience facilitating groups. The four-step process developed over 70 years by the Institute of Cultural Affairs resembled the mediation training I had received. It was grounded in the natural process of human thinking I will talk more about in Chapter 7, Seeing IROD Everywhere.

A couple years into my schooling, I was promoted to an administrator position and attended workshops on restorative practices and restitution (Gossen, 1996). Again, the system employed a four-step process to restore broken or harmed relationships. Strained or broken relationships are a common occurrence in any system with a large concentration of people working together. Restoring the relationship with four simple steps gets participants back on track and moving forward together, often making the relationship stronger than ever.

Each training conveyed slight variations in patterns, vocabulary, and approach, but I noted that each had research-based findings at the core. **And each used four steps.** Each system focused on reaching team decisions, agreements, and consensus. As a leader of teams and groups, I instantly saw the immense value of the science at the core of each process.

I became so intrigued by what caused leaders to succeed or fail that I ended up writing my entire dissertation using overlapping "core leadership science of four" as my theoretical framework (Webb, 2001).

- I chose to study ten high school principals who all attempted to change the daily student schedule to a four-period day—a trending educational strategy of block scheduling with no relationship to the science of four.

- Some leaders succeeded. Several failed. Miserably!

- Curious minds want to know WHY? And I was curious! When I interviewed each principal and overlaid my science of four on top of their stories, the secret of leadership success jumped out.

◆ The principals who succeeded in accomplishing change followed the four steps exactly. By training, experience, or guesswork, they led a process that got results.

◆ When leaders skipped one or more of the four steps in the science of four—they failed. I could demonstrate step by step what went wrong in their implementation.

◆ I realized a life-changing truth. Following this research-based, repeatable pattern would transform my leadership. If I could teach this methodology to others, it would remake their ability to function as **high-performing team members and team leaders**.

The most impactful systems I studied all incorporated the basics of the science of four, leveraging the research that shows how human brains reach decisions. But the jargon in each system was simultaneously too complex and too vague. Hard to follow and even harder to remember.

Over the past many years, I have integrated the key components of these change and decision-making systems into a more manageable, simplified, and memorable process. IROD! The Homerun Leadership process has been influenced by each of these science-based methods for dialogue and decision-making.

By synthesizing and simplifying the four-step science into IROD—

INFORMATION
REACTIONS
OPTIONS
DECISIONS

—leaders can now quickly and easily remember the IROD process and use it immediately.

Everyone I coach wants tools they can immediately use to improve their performance and success. That's always been my goal, too. I wanted something that would change my life and my leadership—fast!

IROD is the secret to achieving leadership success.

I didn't foresee that what I discovered would forever change my leadership and positively impact the lives of everyone who tries IROD and follows the Homerun Basepath. IROD has made me a better leader, a better dad, and a better coach for new leaders.

I work to support others. IROD is super simple. And it's become the gift that keeps on giving.

	IROD Chapter Review Questions
I	What are your key takeaways from this chapter?
R	What reactions do you have to the information shared in this chapter?
O	How did this chapter's ideas offer ways to enhance your decision-making process?
D	What ideas from this chapter could you apply immediately to your team's decision-making?

For bonus video clips, go to **HomerunLeadership.com/Bonus**

CHAPTER 5

My First IROD Homerun

The growth and development of people is the highest calling of leadership.

HARVEY S. FIRESTONE

After five years and $50,000, I completed my doctorate. As I've mentioned, I had moved into administration part way through my program—a shift from classroom Spanish teacher to assistant principal at a high school in the Twin Cities of Minneapolis and St. Paul, Minnesota. This job transition from teacher to assistant principal is the most treacherous shift in public education, as distinct as the shift from Regular Leadership to Homerun Leadership. As a classroom teacher I was able to create a lesson, teach it, and tell the students what homework to complete and when the tests would be. As an administrator, I had to begin working with other team members, to make plans, agreements, and reach consensus based decisions, all day long. What makes the teacher to administrator shift especially challenging is the leadership shift from telling to asking, and from deciding, alone, to reaching consensus, together, with a team.

Upon hearing the news of my doctorate program completion, the superintendent of our school district knocked on my office door and asked if I would be willing to share my learnings at an upcoming district administrative meeting. I was allotted ten minutes.

I wasn't sure how to trim five years and 120 dense pages of research and application into a ten-minute talk, but I ended up bringing a one-page overview of four steps to my presentation.

There's a backstory.

Like most established leaders, once this superintendent had a goal in mind, it was easy for them to skip process steps. They might miss warning signals from people trying to offer insights, the kind of helpful advice that can prevent you from failing. It's important for leaders to remember not to skip steps in the process.

Although I was confident of IROD, the process wasn't previously used by my team to make collaborative decisions. Knowing this made presenting my ideas more than a little intimidating. The IROD process, in fact, is the exact opposite of Regular Leadership.

- IROD is inclusive, and makes room for and respects all voices in the room.
- IROD doesn't force decisions or one particular outcome.
- IROD encourages finding the best team decision to help the organization.

The meeting day arrived, and the superintendent asked me to kick off the meeting with my presentation, before we moved to the main agenda. As I began my ten-minute overview of my doctorate program learnings, I made sure the team understood my one-pager was worth $50,000. I explained my discovery that teams function better in decision-making situations when they follow a four-step process.

The key is asking four questions, in order, and allowing time and space for the team to give their best feedback and ideas. When teams create this opening, they can harness all the team's best ideas and leave the meeting with the best team decision.

My one-pager looked something like this. You've already previewed it in the Three Quick Hits section of this book:

The Best Problem-Solving and Decision-Making Framework for your next agenda item:			
INITIAL	**BASE**	**QUESTION**	**CLEAN-UP QUESTION**
I	1st	Do we have all the INFORMATION on this topic?	Anything else?
R	2nd	Do we have everyone's REACTIONS to the information?	Anything else?
O	3rd	Have we brainstormed all the OPTIONS, listed pros and cons of each, and prioritized the list?	Anything else?
D	4th	Is the DECISION the will of the group?	Anything else?

(Conbere, 1996; Spencer, 1989; Stanfield, 1997; "Technology of Participation," n.d.)

After I finished, the superintendent thanked me and said, "Let's use Dave's Homerun framework to work through our next issue on our agenda—the curriculum decision." I was excited, honored, and shocked they took my overview and willingly applied it to our team meeting. They gave it a shot as a different way to work through difficult issues.

Back then, my IROD language and presentation wasn't nearly as stream-lined as it is now. Nevertheless, ten minutes and a one-page introduc-tion was all these leaders needed to begin to understand and apply the process. One by one, the superintendent led the team through the IROD questions. In order:

- **At 1st base,** the superintendent asked for all the INFORMATION about the curriculum issue. Our curriculum director and elementary principal shared details regarding a reading program and the challenges they faced. The superintendent asked the 1st base question multiple times until nobody answered, then moved to 2nd base.

- **At 2nd base,** the superintendent asked if anyone had any REACTIONS to the information shared. Several people explained their reactions, and as they continued to ask for more reactions, soon no one else shared, and they moved to 3rd base.

- **At 3rd base,** the superintendent asked the team to brainstorm OPTIONS that could help solve this team problem. We used a flip chart on a stand at the front of the team, and as options were shared, I listed them on the chart, allowing the options to remain visible for the team. The team shared three different ideas, and as the superintendent asked, "Anything else?" it was clear we had run out of other ideas.

  Continuing at the flip chart, we then listed pros and cons of each brainstormed item to the right of each option. When the superintendent asked us to prioritize the list based on these pros and cons, it was clear from our flip chart work that option two was the most viable and most likely the will of the group.

- **At 4th base,** the superintendent asked, "Is option #2 the will of the group?" What had started as two different perspectives on our reading program had now merged into one clear direction and vision for our district. A DECISION! It was a huge Homerun for the superintendent, the team, and our school district with just four IROD questions—and it almost looked like nothing happened because the process of decision-making was so smooth.

After the team meeting, I asked the elementary principal how they thought the reading discussion went. "That was the first time the curriculum director listened to my perspective in three years," the principal said. Homerun and then some!

This process brought a quiet win, healing, and restoration to a relationship strained for years. By listening to all team voices, you can accomplish the same. You not only harness the gifts and strengths of every team member, but you also support your people to work better together and rebuild trust and confidence in each other and the team.

In this true story, a simple framework and basic IROD questions demonstrate how you can have an immediate, major, positive impact in your next meeting or your next big decision. By slowing down and following this process, you will ensure that

- All information is collected and shared.
- All reactions are heard.
- All options are listed and weighed.
- The best decision can be made.

The result of following this process will likely be a quiet win—like the story I just shared—and wins whether large or small are all Homeruns, because you win together.

To sum up this story, a Regular Leader asked the four questions in order, applying the strategy and framework perfectly to make leadership look and feel easy.

You can do the same. As you begin utilizing this framework and these questions, you begin the shift from Regular Leadership to Homerun Leadership.

Homerun Leadership isn't about a single style, personality, area of expertise, or skill set. Everyone can be a Homerun Leader. The goal is to follow a good, proven process inclusive of all team members to reach the best decision.

Want to make the shift to Homerun Leadership? It's attainable by any leader. Keep reading.

	IROD Chapter Review Questions
I	What are your key takeaways from this chapter?
R	What reactions do you have to the information shared in this chapter?
O	How did this chapter's ideas offer ways to enhance your decision-making process?
D	What ideas from this chapter could you apply immediately to your team's decision-making?

For bonus video clips, go to **HomerunLeadership.com/Bonus**

CHAPTER 6

Regular Leadership vs. Homerun Leadership

If everyone is moving forward together,
then success takes care of itself.

HENRY FORD

As a Homerun Leadership coach, the leaders I advise approach their role with good intentions. But they're often unhappy with their results. They do their best to encourage the team to work together towards an agreement, but the team is frustrated, angry, and distrustful of each other. They're stressed out!

They are Regular Leaders doing Regular Leadership.

I call it "Regular Leadership" because it's what we see everywhere we look. In Regular Leadership, when a tough problem arises and the team lacks a good process or structure for resolving the issue, it's not uncommon for the team to revert to blaming, shaming, disagreement, and dissonance. This discord is born from different interpretations of the issue and differing approaches to solving the problem.

The result is that we can find ourselves in a room with the brightest and most engaged folks around—with a problem that needs to be solved—but no one can agree on a path forward. Even if there's a designated path, there's often dissonance among the team about why it's the right path to follow. And the discord can linger and create lasting negative team dynamics.

Our response as leaders to that normal team tension is the difference between Regular Leadership and Homerun Leadership.

© 2020 Ted Goff

"...and if we all talk really fast at the same time we'll get much more done."

Regular Leadership
(inevitably furthering team disagreement)

Leaders do their best with what they know. When a tough team problem arises, Regular Leaders feel stressed and attempt to solve the issue quickly. However, their snap decisions often make the problem worse, requiring follow-up and clean-up that takes more time than leading with a good decision-making process from the start.

Regular Leaders lack knowledge of the critical steps of good problem-solving and decision-making, so they revert to telling others what to do rather than collaborating with others to develop the best plans and decisions. When leaders skip key steps of good process, they weaken team support, team confidence, and the overall team decision or plan.

Homerun Leadership
(a repeatable process facilitating team agreement)

When a tough team problem or issue arises on their agenda, Homerun Leaders stick to the core leadership science of four and patterns found in the IROD steps. They use a problem-solving and decision-making framework to work through the issue. Homerun Leaders ask for team input to develop great team plans and agreements. When leaders follow key steps of good process, they increase team support, team confidence, and team success.

Here's another look to help you quickly discern the difference between Regular Leaders and Homerun Leaders:

Regular Leaders vs. Homerun Leaders

Regular Leaders make decisions independently without gathering all the information or allowing the team to react and research alternative options, creating mistrust and resistance.	Homerun Leaders gather the best information, the team's reactions to this information, brainstorm together and prioritize possible options to reach a team decision.
• **A**ssume team vision (MY way) • **T**ell others what to do • **D**iscourage input • **P**romote team resistance and tension • **D**ecrease team trust • **C**reate win/lose situations • **Fight**	• **D**evelop team vision (OUR way) • **D**evelop plans together • **A**sk for input • **P**romote team acceptance and support • **I**ncrease team trust • **C**reate team wins • **Facilitate**

HOMERUN LEADERS lead BETTER and lead FASTER by moving people together toward mutually agreed-upon goals.

When you are intentional about following the IROD framework as your team faces a problem or needs to reach a decision—a situation that happens hourly in the world of a school district superintendent, where almost any incident or conflict between a student, parent, teacher, or community member has the potential to become front page news—you dramatically increase your odds of success (your batting average) rather than distress, and team agreement rather than disagreement.

I know you have a vision in your mind of the kind of leader you want to be. Someone who creates forward momentum. I also know that you're frustrated when reality doesn't match this vision. You want to do better and just wish you knew how.

Homerun Leadership naturally harnesses the skills, knowledge, expertise, ideas, and innovation of each member on your team, including you. It's built into the system.

When everything goes great, you might temporarily get by without a system. But when the going gets tough, you need Homerun Leadership.

This information will help you begin your shift from
Regular Leadership to Homerun Leadership
Regular Teams to Homerun Teams
Distress to success
Disagreement to agreement.

That's a HOMERUN!

	IROD Chapter Review Questions
I	What are your key takeaways from this chapter?
R	What reactions do you have to the information shared in this chapter?
O	How did this chapter's ideas offer ways to enhance your decision-making process?
D	What ideas from this chapter could you apply immediately to your team's decision making?

For bonus video clips, go to **HomerunLeadership.com/Bonus**

CHAPTER 7

See IROD Everywhere

A leader is one who knows the way, goes the way, and shows the way.

JOHN MAXWELL

I became a believer in IROD science when I began noticing its patterns proven in real life. For you to make the shift from Regular Leadership to Homerun Leadership, you too need to experience IROD in action. I know that as soon as you grasp the basics of IROD, you'll recognize its patterns *everywhere*.

The classic book by Stanfield (1997), *The Art of Focused Conversation*, offers an overview of the natural method that highlights an example of how you likely use the four-step method without even knowing it. I use an abbreviated version of his example for this coaching point.

Imagine you're driving to work. You approach an intersection, and the light turns yellow.

"Ohhhh, shoot!"

In that instant, you can either:

- Step on the gas and speed through the intersection, OR
- Hit the brakes and come to a stop.

What did you decide?

I admit it. I hit the gas.

I assume you've faced that situation once or twice in your driving experience. Maybe once or twice today. Even if you're a super safety-minded driver.

But let's look at the event again, this time breaking it down into IROD steps:

IROD	IROD Story
INFORMATION	1 – You're in your car, driving to work. As you approach an intersection, the light turns yellow.
REACTIONS	2 – You say, "Ohhhh, shoot!!"
OPTIONS	3 – You can either step on the gas and speed through the intersection or hit the brakes and come to a stop. You quickly examine the pros and cons of each option.
DECISION	4 – You ran the light or came to a stop.

Let's run through that scenario yet again, but this time as I tell the story I want you to follow along by holding up one, two, three, or four fingers, depending on which base we're at. Teachers and trainers call this "pattern recognition practice."

If the point in the story is an INFORMATION piece, hold up one finger. If we're at REACTIONS, hold up two fingers, and so on.

Here's the story again.

- Picture yourself driving to work. (You should be holding up one finger.)
- As you approach an intersection, the light turns yellow. Ohhhhh, shoot!
- You realize you can either step on the gas and speed through the intersection or hit the brakes and come to a stop. You quickly examine the pros and cons of each option.
- You decide and act.

Did you hold up the correct number of fingers for 1st, 2nd, 3rd, or 4th base—for INFORMATION, REACTIONS, OPTIONS, and DECISION?

Countless variations to the four-step process can happen when you approach a real-life intersection. They can cause you to shift quickly between IROD steps and ultimately cause you to make a different decision:

- Just as you step on the gas, you spot a police car. That new information causes you to reevaluate the pros and cons of running the light. I don't know about you, but I always make a quick decision to slam the brakes and avoid a ticket.

- You glance at the time and realize you're five minutes behind schedule. New information prompts a stronger reaction. You step on the gas and get through the intersection, hoping to make up time.

These variations aren't exceptions to the IROD rule. They help demonstrate the four-step process. Each time you acquire new information, your brain restarts IROD. To incorporate new information into the decision-making process, you go back to the first step.

The same situation happens frequently on teams when you get new information. And problems result when you don't back up in the process!

This stoplight example isn't the only scenario that validates the four-step process. It's just one of many examples that makes it easy to see and feel the science of IROD.

If you consider all the situations you face in a day, you will recognize this pattern in each of them. Deciding what to wear in the morning, what to eat for lunch, or what to pack for your upcoming vacation—each situation follows the same four steps to a decision. Although you're rarely consciously aware of this natural flow, all your decisions follow this pattern: INFORMATION, REACTIONS, OPTIONS, and DECISION.

	IROD Chapter Review Questions
I	What are your key takeaways from this chapter?
R	What reactions do you have to the information shared in this chapter?
O	How did this chapter's ideas offer ways to enhance your decision-making process?
D	What ideas from this chapter could you apply immediately to your team's decision-making?

For bonus video clips, go to **HomerunLeadership.com/Bonus**

CHAPTER 8

IROD Basics

A problem clearly stated is a problem half solved.

DOROTHEA BRANDE

To begin to see and feel the science of change and decision-making, you need to be rock-solid on these IROD basics. Don't try to slide by this point. Everything builds from here.

The first challenge is to simply memorize what the I, R, O, and D each stand for:

I	INFORMATION
R	REACTIONS
O	OPTIONS
D	DECISIONS

Run through that list—**IROD**—a few times. Out loud. You want to be able to rattle off these terms as easily as saying your name. Now, without looking at the chart above, can you fill in the chart below?

I	I _____
R	R _____
O	O _____
D	D _____

The next challenge is to learn to fill in the four bases so you can connect IROD to the bases on the baseball diamond. This will give you a ready visual reference as you lead and run good process—as you "run the base-path" with your team:

1st Base	I	INFORMATION
2nd Base	R	REACTIONS
3rd Base	O	OPTIONS
4th Base	D	DECISIONS

Without looking at the chart above, can you fill in the remainder of this chart?

1st		
		REACTIONS
	O	

Next, you want to build your skills and ask the **IROD Homerun** questions. In this challenge, you need to be able to fill in the four questions that equip you to facilitate running the bases (running good process) with your team:

1st	I	INFORMATION	Do we have all the INFORMATION?
2nd	R	REACTIONS	Do we have everyone's REACTIONS to the information?
3rd	O	OPTIONS	Have we brainstormed all the OPTIONS, listed pros and cons of each and prioritized the list?
4th	D	DECISIONS	Is the DECISION the will of the group?

Can you fill in the rest of the chart below to match the chart above? Do your best!

	I		
2nd			
			Have we brainstormed all the OPTIONS, listed pros and cons of each and prioritized the list?
		DECISIONS	

After you've asked each of these four Homerun questions, there's a single Cleanup question for you to ask following each: "Anything else?" This is the best question ever to ensure you've fully completed each base.

If someone answers your question, continue to ask, "Anything else?" until you get silence. "Crickets are your ticket" to the next base.

Here's a fully completed chart that includes the bases, the initials, the key words, the Homerun questions as well as your Cleanup question at each base. Using this chart will help you activate and follow the simplified science to facilitate decision-making with your team:

1st	I	INFORMATION	Do we have all the INFORMATION?	Anything else?
2nd	R	REACTIONS	Do we have everyone's REACTIONS to the information?	Anything else?
3rd	O	OPTIONS	Have we brainstormed all the OPTIONS, listed pros and cons of each and prioritized the list?	Anything else?
4th	D	DECISIONS	Is the DECISION the will of the group?	Anything else?

Can you fill in the remainder of this chart to match the chart above, without looking at the chart above? Do your best!

1st				Anything else?
		REACTIONS		
	O			
			Is the DECISION the will of the group?	

I want to be clear about the order of the questions. The IROD order matters. So does ensuring you have fully completed each base. I'll explain more about this later when we get to the Team Leadership Types section, highlighting the need to fully meet the needs of each Leadership Type.

In this next chart, I've numbered each question, 1 thru 8, spelling out each question to ask to run the bases with your team.

1. Do we have all the INFORMATION?	2. Anything else?
3. Do we have everyone's REACTIONS to the information?	4. Anything else?
5. Have we brainstormed all the OPTIONS, listed pros and cons of each and prioritized the list?	6. Anything else?
7. Is the DECISION the will of the group?	8. Anything else?

Here is another view of the same order:

1.	Do we have all the INFORMATION?
2.	Anything else?
3.	Do we have everyone's REACTIONS to the information?
4.	Anything else?
5.	Have we brainstormed all the OPTIONS, listed pros and cons of each and prioritized the list?
6.	Anything else?
7.	Is the DECISION the will of the group?
8.	Anything else?

Here's your final challenge. Without looking at the chart above, can you complete the chart below?

1.	Do we have all the _____?
2.	Anything _____?

3.	Do we have _____ _____ to the information?
4.	_____ _____?
5.	Have we brainstormed all the _____, listed _____ and _____ of each and prioritized the list?
6.	_____ else?
7.	Is _____ _____ the will of the group?
8.	_____ _____?

Once you have these eight great questions memorized—all based on IROD—you now know enough to be dangerous. When you find a problem to apply it to, you'll see the power for yourself!

	IROD Chapter Review Questions
I	What are your key takeaways from this chapter?
R	What reactions do you have to the information shared in this chapter?
O	How did this chapter's ideas offer ways to enhance your decision-making process?
D	What ideas from this chapter could you apply immediately to your team's decision-making?

For bonus video clips, go to **HomerunLeadership.com/Bonus**

CHAPTER 9

Know Your Leadership Gifts and Gaps

Homerun Leadership Types Assessment

Knowing yourself is the beginning of all wisdom.

ARISTOTLE

Back in chapter three, you took a one-question quiz that highlighted your Homerun Leadership Type. You likely quickly recognized yourself in one of the types, and you've had several chapters to test that discovery and glimpse how it might play out as you lead.

I want to introduce you now to the real Homerun Leadership Types Assessment. Being certain about your own type is crucial, because that preference affects your decision-making in team situations.

Once you master your own type, you'll start to recognize how crucial all four Homerun Team Leadership Types are to managing good process and team decision-making in the people around you. You'll also find you begin to place greater value on the gifts other people bring to your team—in particular, their approach to decision-making. They see things from a different vantage point, and that's incredibly valuable!

Some of your teammates may frustrate you. As Homerun Leadership principles help you understand their approach to decision-making, your appreciation for your opposite types will increase. You'll discover your own gaps and blind spots. At least I did.

In the end, you'll know exactly what each person on your team needs to feel good about your team decisions.

You can discover your Homerun Leadership Type with this 20-question quiz (adapted from "School Reform Initiative," 2017), followed by a self-scoring guide.

By the way, this assessment is research-based, revealing, and reliable—and it's equally useful for leaders and team members. Complete this quick assessment now, because all the Homerun Leadership strategies depend on you identifying your own approach to decisions.

The Homerun Leadership Types Assessment

Answer the 20 questions below to help you identify your Homerun Leadership Type. Don't overthink it. Go with your first response. Using Y for YES, and N for NO, mark the following short self assessment. Answer quickly but carefully with your gut instinct, focused on the context of how you make decisions. As you mark your answers, keep in mind that there are no wrong answers here, just different personality styles.

At the end of the assessment, score your answers and compare them to the chart in the next section.

		YES	NO
1.	I am very detail-oriented.		
2.	I am very caring and understanding.		
3.	I consider all my options before deciding.		
4.	I jump in and act.		
5.	I need to know the who/what/where/when/why before making a decision.		
6.	I am very inclusive of others, in order to make the best plans.		
7.	I am an idea person.		
8.	I like to get started.		
9.	I need to know all the information before deciding.		
10.	I am thoughtful of others' perspectives before moving ahead.		
11.	I make lists of all the possibilities and choices.		
12.	I get restless and impatient when others have a hard time deciding.		
13.	I have a hard time deciding without all the facts.		
14.	I ensure all voices are heard in order to make better decisions.		
15.	I am always searching for a better or the best idea.		
16.	I can decide without all the information, feedback, or options.		
17.	I am thorough and comprehensive in my approach.		
18.	I am a good listener, because I want the input of others.		
19.	I have difficulty making a decision if there are multiple options available.		
20.	I am impulsive or fast paced.		

Homerun Leadership Types Assessment Results

Congratulations! You've just completed the Homerun Leadership Types Assessment.

Now that you've taken the test, take a minute to score yourself based on your answers.

STEP 1: From the Homerun Team Leadership Types Assessment above, transfer your results to the chart below, giving yourself 1 point for each YES response and 0 points for each NO response.

STEP 2: Add up the numbers in each column to determine your Homerun Team Leadership Types scores from 0-5 (with 0 being low and 5 being high). There are no right or wrong scores, only your scores. All Homerun Types are a gift to your team!

THE FOUR HOMERUN LEADERSHIP TYPES			
1st Baser **INFORMATION**	**2nd Baser** **REACTIONS**	**3rd Baser** **OPTIONS**	**4th Baser** **DECISION**
1. _____	2. _____	3. _____	4. _____
5. _____	6. _____	7. _____	8. _____
9. _____	10. _____	11. _____	12. _____
13. _____	14. _____	15. _____	16. _____
17. _____	18. _____	19. _____	20. _____
Column Total _____ **out of 5**	**Column Total** _____ **out of 5**	**Column Total** _____ **out of 5**	**Column Total** _____ **out of 5**

The category with the most points from your self-assessment is your predominant Homerun Leadership Type. It's the approach that most commonly comes out when you're in a decision-making situation. When your team is in a decision-making situation, it's how you show up.

Your Leadership Type:

- Drives your *motivations* and *behavior.*
- Makes you *feel* good about a decision.
- Makes you *think* a decision is correct.

Your Leadership Type is what you care about most in a decision-making situation. If you have equal or nearly equal points in more than one category, that's completely normal. It implies you inherently have multiple priorities in making decisions.

The higher you score on any of these "bases," the stronger your gifts in that area. A high score on any given base indicates that this area is especially important for you to complete in order to be satisfied with a decision.

The lower you score on any base, the lower your strengths are in that area. A low score on any given base indicates a need for support in that area from other team members.

Using your results from the assessment chart, take a moment to rank them in order from highest to lowest using the chart below. For example, my ranked results look like this:

Dave's LEADERSHIP TYPE Scores (ranked high to low)	
Leadership Type 1st baser, 2nd baser, 3rd baser, 4th baser	**Total Points Scored**
4th Baser DECISION	5 points
3rd Baser OPTIONS	3 points
2nd Baser REACTIONS	2 points
1st Baser INFORMATION	0 points

My LEADERSHIP TYPE Scores (ranked high to low)	
Leadership Type 1st baser, 2nd baser, 3rd baser, 4th baser	**Total Points Scored**
_____ Baser	_____ points
_____ Baser	_____ points
_____ Baser	_____ points
_____ Baser	_____ points

The Leadership Types Assessment is designed to help you understand what priorities you consciously or unconsciously bring to a team decision-making process and to highlight that everyone else on the team brings a personality priority, or leadership focus, to the table that may be different than yours. When we recognize our own preference and acknowledge that preference in others, then we can work the Homerun Leadership system to reach a team decision.

Remember: Your Homerun Leadership Type isn't good, bad, or something in-between. It's simply how you and your teammates show up and react/

behave when facing a team decision. There are no good or bad results. They're just results.

Everyone has a Leadership Type. And there's not a "right" baser to be. All are very special. (Well, isn't that special?)

When your team embarks on a decision-making process, your Homerun Team Leadership Type shows up. The higher your score in a certain area, the more it appears at the meeting.

It's not uncommon for you to score high in more than one area. It's also not uncommon to score a zero in one or more areas. If you score high in an area, that's where you focus in a decision-making situation. It comes naturally to you. If you scored lower in any area, this indicates this "base" isn't as important to you in how you make your decisions.

As you look at your Leadership Type scores, examine both your strengths and areas where you might be missing something—your areas of opportunity.

If you scored a zero in a particular Homerun Leadership Type area, like I did, this book will help you to grow your leadership proficiency in that area. You want to fill your gaps because the secret recipe of good team decision-making is completing the information, and meeting the needs, at each of the 4 bases. Most likely, you have someone on your team who scored high in that certain type, and this book will teach you how to effectively work alongside that teammate to achieve greater results.

	IROD Chapter Review Questions
I	What are your key takeaways from this chapter?
R	What reactions do you have to the information shared in this chapter?
O	How did this chapter's ideas offer ways to enhance your decision-making process?
D	What ideas from this chapter could you apply immediately to your team's decision-making?

For bonus video clips, go to **HomerunLeadership.com/Bonus**

CHAPTER 10

Recognize Leadership Types at Team Meetings

Team leaders have to connect with their team and them-selves. If they don't know their team's strengths and weak-nesses, they cannot hand off responsibilities to the team. And if they don't know their own strengths and weakness-es, they will not hand off responsibilities to the team.

JOHN C. MAXWELL

For each base along the Homerun Leadership Basepath, there is a corre-sponding Homerun Leadership Type, an approach to decision-making that prioritizes one piece of IROD: Information, Reactions, Options, or Decisions.

In practical terms, not everyone has the same priorities in mind when reaching a decision:

- Some people are most concerned with knowing they have every piece of information available before making the decision.
- Some people want to know how everyone affected by the decision will feel about it.
- Some people care most about ensuring they know all the options before reaching a final decision.

- Some people just want to reach a decision and are willing to make it with whatever information and options are available at that time.

Here are those ideas in chart form:

I	R	O	D
1st Basers have a high need for:	2nd Basers have a high need for:	3rd Basers have a high need for:	4th Basers have a high need for:
• Information • Facts • Data • Details	• Reactions • Reflections • Feelings • Feedback	• Options • Ideas • Choices • Possibilities	• Decisions • Agreements • Plans • Recommenda-tions

Our individual Homerun Leadership Type determines how we show up in decision-making situations—our most dominant personality pops up. And odds are high that in any meeting, there will be people present with different Leadership Types.

Don't miss what this means. While MY Leadership Type dictates how I show up in decision-making situations, this same is true of all the other people on a team. Their Leadership Types determine how THEY show up in the decision-making process, and their needs may be different than mine.

Each Type brings a different set of needs and priorities to meetings, and the Types present determine the dynamics of meetings.

**Knowing the four Homerun Leadership Types—
and how to meet the needs of each Type—
can make or break a team's success.**

As I look around my most effective leadership teams, I realize I've surrounded myself with leaders representing all four Leadership Types. That's the ideal. The presence of each Type is important, because each leader brings a different perspective to the decision-making process. Together we reach stronger, more successful decisions.

We're all biased toward leading with our own Homerun Leadership Type. It's only natural. However, the best leaders I know make time to address the needs of each Leadership Type—in the specific IROD order—to reach shared decisions supported by the whole group. That's a Homerun!

The opposite is also true. Leaders who fail to follow the science-based process of Information, Reactions, Options, Decision may make decisions that satisfy their own needs but neglect the interests of others. That's a strikeout!

Let me illustrate that point now with four scenarios. In chapter 11, I'll show you the same meeting led by each of the four Homerun Leadership Types, where the leader misses the opportunity to meet the needs of other Types. In chapter 12, I'll provide a final example of the same meeting, this time where the leader uses the IROD process, appreciating and including all perspectives to reach great decisions.

	IROD Chapter Review Questions
I	What are your key takeaways from this chapter?
R	What reactions do you have to the information shared in this chapter?
O	How did this chapter's ideas offer ways to enhance your decision-making process?
D	What ideas from this chapter could you apply immediately to your team's decision-making?

For bonus video clips, go to **HomerunLeadership.com/Bonus**

CHAPTER 11

Homerun Leadership Types Scenarios—Four Strikeouts

In most cases, strengths and weaknesses are two sides of the same coin. A strength in one situation is a weakness in another, yet often the person can't switch gears. It's a very subtle thing to talk about strengths and weaknesses because almost always they're the same thing.

STEVE JOBS

To see Homerun Leadership Type in action, let's watch the same meeting led by each of the four Leadership Types. In the first four scenarios, a leader representing one of the four Types will take charge without considering the needs of other Types. In the final example, the leader will use the IROD process to include all perspectives and reach a great decision.

The issue at hand is the reduction of a school district budget by half a million dollars. No small challenge, and an example of problems faced by leadership teams everywhere.

SCENARIO 1: The Budget Reduction Meeting Led by 1st Base Leadership Type—Ian Information

A week prior to a meeting focused on significant cost reductions, Ian Information sends the team an extensive set of budget-related documents for review—a predictable move given Ian's preference for information-based decisions. Ian believes that delivering necessary information ahead of time guarantees the team meeting will be efficient and effective.

As a Homerun Leadership Type 1st Baser, Ian Information focuses on facts and details. His Type loves detail, comprehensive research, and sees gathering all the data as the most important part of making great decisions.

With Ian at the lead, the meeting unfolds:

> **Ian Information:** "Our goal today is to determine budget reductions for this year. We'll begin by reviewing our budget data. By fully grounding ourselves in our current financial state, our options will be clear, and we'll make the best decision possible."

Ian Information leads the team through revenue and expenditure reports, current budget projections, budget assumptions, and budget recommendations. At a meeting scheduled for an hour and a half, presenting information takes a full hour. As everyone realizes only a half hour remains, the team feels pressure to reach a quick decision.

> **Ian Information:** "Ok, everybody. Let's decide how we plan to remove $500,000 from our budget."

Dave Decider jumps in right away.

Dave Decider: "Well, if we just extend our walking distance to our schools, that will allow us to reduce our busing budget by approximately $100,000. That leaves just $400,000 left to cut. Then, if we raise class sizes at the elementary and secondary schools, we could eliminate five teachers, saving approximately $400,000 and getting us close to our goal. Does that sound good to everyone? I'd be okay if we just did this plan."

Ian Information: "We need to stay focused on the facts and data our decision will be based on. We can't just jump to a decision without knowing all the information."

Rita Reactions: "Dave, we can't do that. Our teachers would come unglued if they're the only ones reduced district-wide. We haven't even surveyed our staff to ask what reductions they might recommend this year."

Ian Information: "We have to make a decision, Rita, and we can't afford the time or effort it would require getting input from everyone affected."

Olivia Options: "There have to be other ideas we could consider we haven't thought of yet. I wonder if we could spread the cuts out among all staff in the district, or maybe we could increase our revenue by asking voters for a tax increase rather than cutting our budgets."

Ian Information responds by encouraging his team to stay focused on details and information and throws cold water on Olivia's ideas.

Ian Information: "By going back to all our information and data, we'll have a clear path for the team to follow and won't need to waste time creating a list of options."

Ian Information also shares why Olivia's brainstormed ideas won't work.

Ian Information: "Even if we went out to the community for a tax levy referendum, the dollars wouldn't arrive in the district until the following year, so we would still need to reduce our budgets for this year by $500,000. So now what do you want to do?"

Dave Decider: "Well, if you all don't like my teacher reduction idea, we could just reduce our classroom assistants—cutting fewer teachers—and spread this more evenly around the district, so not just teachers are targeted."

Ian Information: "Sorry, Dave, we can't make a decision like that without further analysis of the data."

Rita Reactions: "There's got to be a better way. Everyone is going to get super upset if we just go this direction."

Ian Information: "Sorry, Rita, we can't please everyone. We just have to make a decision based on the data we have."

Olivia Options: "I think we should list all the options of things we could cut to find the best option—or we won't make the best choice."

Ian Information: "Olivia, we don't need to review every possibility. We only need to rely on the data, and it will be clear which decision is best."

Dave Decider: "I have another meeting starting shortly. I'm sorry but I need to leave. I also have to say I'm frustrated we couldn't just make a decision today."

Ian Information: "Okay, we didn't get to a decision today, but we need to make this decision this week. I'll send out another meeting request.

Please review the information and data that you've been given and come to the next meeting with your best budget- reduction ideas."

Looks like the team is hung up without an answer to a pressing issue. That's a strikeout!

SCENARIO 2: The Budget Reduction Meeting Led By 2nd Base Leadership Type—Rita Reactions

At this budget meeting, Rita Reactions serves as team leader. Her 2nd Base Leadership Type focuses on feedback and input from others. Her Type truly cares about the thoughts and feelings of others, so she focuses on gathering everyone's perspectives, feedback, reactions, and reflections, believing that the best decisions are made when all voices are heard in the process. She's caring and highly sensitive to the feelings of all.

With Rita at the lead, the meeting gets underway:

Rita Reactions: "Everybody, I have extremely bad news for you today. I'm so sorry to have to share this, but the board has decided that we need to cut $500,000 from our budget. I realize this is a bombshell, but with the support and encouragement of everyone on this team, we can get through this together. Our goal is to decide today those budget reductions for the coming school year. I want to take time to hear from all of you before we make our final decision. To get us started, let's go around the table and hear your thoughts and reactions to this difficult news."

Dave Decider: "Well, I don't like this, but if the board made this decision, we have to make ours. So if we just extend our walking distance to our schools, that would be approximately $100,000 in reduced transportation costs. That leaves just $400,000 to cut. Then, if we just raise class sizes at the elementary and secondary schools, we could eliminate five teachers and get us close to our goal."

Rita Reactions: "We can't make a drastic decision like that without talking to the parents who would be affected by the increased walking distance for their children. We would also need to hear the voices of the teachers and parents who would be affected by the larger class sizes."

Olivia Options: "There have to be other ideas than just those two ideas. We should consider ideas we haven't thought of yet. I wonder if we could spread the cuts out among all staff in the district. Or another idea—rather than cutting our budgets—might be to increase revenue by asking voters for a tax increase. If we just all list our ideas, we could come up with the best option and work through this challenge."

Rita Reactions: "With either of those choices, we could face serious pushback and unhappiness from our staff and the public. We can't afford that risk. I'm just not comfortable with unvetted ideas."

Ian Information: "Even if we went to the community for an increased tax levy referendum this fall, the dollars wouldn't arrive in the district until the following year, so we would still need to reduce our budgets for this year by $500,000. I think we should slow down and take time to review the entire budget. By doing this, we understand the facts and ultimately better identify possible areas for reductions."

Rita Reactions: "Well, I feel we should survey our staff to ask what reductions they might recommend this year. I think if we get their input and feedback, we will get ideas that could serve us well in making our reduction decisions."

Rita shares that she is ending this meeting early and scheduling another meeting, so that she can create a brief all-staff budget survey to get feedback to this team to inform the final budget-reduction ideas.

Dave Decider: "Well, if you all don't like my teacher-reduction idea, I think we could just reduce the number of our classroom assistants—cutting fewer teachers—and spread this evenly around the district. Then not just teachers would be targeted."

Rita Reactions: "It would be even worse to reduce staff all around the district. Far more people would be affected. I think they would revolt."

Olivia Options: "I think a survey could help us create a list of all the potential reductions."

Rita Reactions: "That's a good idea, but we need to make sure we get input from all the potentially affected parties as we create this survey. We need to make sure everyone gets their say and nobody feels left out."

Dave Decider: "I'm frustrated we couldn't decide today. It's clear where we can make cuts."

Rita Reactions: "Well, we didn't get to a decision today, but we need to make a decision this week. I'll send another meeting invitation so we can continue to work on this problem. I'll share the results of the survey, and I want you to come prepared for the next meeting with your best budget-reduction ideas based on those results. Thanks, everyone!"

As the team leaves the room, Olivia and Ian head to their offices. On the way, each shares their frustration with the meeting.

Olivia Options: "If we had just brainstormed all the possible budget-reduction ideas, we would know what's best. We could have generated ideas, narrowed the list, and left with a plan."

Ian Information: "The staff survey is fine, but they aren't grounded in the budget details. The staff and the board count on us to keep an eye on those facts. I'm frustrated and afraid that we'll end up making a decision without all the data we need. Ugh! I sure hope at the next meeting we get grounded on all of the facts."

Olivia Options: "Yeah, that would help us get to the best options for decision-making, too. See you, Ian."

No decision. No satisfaction with the process or outcome. That's a strikeout!

© 2020 Ted Goff

"When I asked for ideas about how I could be a better boss, I didn't want so many."

SCENARIO 3: The Budget Reduction Meeting Led By 3rd Base Leadership Type—Olivia Options

As this budget meeting begins, Olivia Options is team leader. Olivia's Homerun Leadership Type values gathering and brainstorming all the best options and ideas. Her Type also likes to investigate and debate the pros and cons of each option to ensure the best option is ultimately selected. 3rd Basers feel most supported by team conversation, which helps narrow the list of brainstormed ideas to find the right plan and the best way forward.

> **Olivia Options:** "OK, everybody, let's decide today what our budget reductions will be for this year. To get us moving, I want us to brainstorm a list of reduction ideas that will get us to our goal."

> **Ian Information:** "Before we jump to brainstorming, Olivia, shouldn't we check for questions on the budget information I sent to the team? I would be happy to walk you through each budget point to get the team fully grounded."

> **Olivia Options:** "We could, but I think that each of us has worked with this budget for years, so I'm not sure how much use that would be. We know the board has asked us to decrease our budget by $500,000. It's best just to move into discussing options to reach our goal. Everybody, let's get all our ideas up on the board for everyone to see and follow along."

> **Dave Decider:** "If we just extend our walking distance to our schools, that will save $100,000 because we would need fewer buses. That leaves just $400,000 left to cut. We could easily raise class sizes at the elementary and secondary schools to eliminate five teachers and get us close to our goal."

Olivia Options: "Great, Dave. I got it. Thanks. Let's write these two options on the board in front of us. Who else has ideas?"

Dave Decider: "Wait, let's talk about my ideas before we go on to anything else. It's the right decision and might be our only option. I think we should just go with this and be done."

Olivia Options: "Dave, in brainstorming, we need to consider ALL the options before we make a decision. Like they always say, there's no bad idea in brainstorming, so let's go get more ideas to add to our options. I wonder if we could spread the cuts out among all staff in the district, or maybe we could forgo the cuts and increase revenue by asking our voters for a tax increase."

Rita Reactions: "For sure, we can't do the teacher-reduction idea. Our teachers would come unglued if they are the only ones reduced. We haven't even surveyed our staff to ask what reductions they might recommend this year."

Olivia Options: "Rita, we can't afford to consider people's feelings when we're brainstorming. We just need to list all the options, regardless of how they might impact others. Let's stay focused on generating ideas and possible options to solve our budget challenge."

Ian Information: "This decision needs to be based on the data. I don't think we fully understand the data yet—and what it's telling us."

Olivia Options: "The data is helpful, Ian, but right now we need to list all our options. What would you like to add?"

Dave Decider: "If you all don't like my teacher-reduction idea, I think we could just reduce the number of our classroom assistants—cutting fewer teachers—and spread this evenly around the district. Then more than teachers would be targeted. You can add that to the list, but we all know we're going to have to cut either teachers or classroom assistants."

Olivia Options: "OK, Dave, let's add that new option of reducing classroom assistants to the list, and I disagree that it's either one or the other. We have a lot of options we haven't explored yet."

Rita Reactions: "There's got to be a better way. Everyone is going to get super upset if we just go this direction. Could we at least survey the staff to get their input?"

Olivia Options: "I'll add a survey idea to the list of brainstorms, just so we don't lose that thought, but again, this isn't a district-wide staff decision. It's up to this leadership team to reduce the budget."

Dave Decider: "I have another meeting starting, and I'm sorry, but I have to leave. I'm frustrated we couldn't decide today."

Olivia Options: "We didn't get to a decision today, but we need a decision this week. I'll send another meeting invite and we'll try again. Please come to the next meeting with at least three new budget-reduction ideas to add to our list. Thanks, everyone!"

Frustration on all sides. No resolution. Another strikeout!

SCENARIO 4: The Budget Reduction Meeting Led By 4th Base Leadership Type—Dave Decider

In this budget meeting scenario, Dave Decider is the team leader. His Homerun Leadership Type focuses on deciding, acting, and compelling movement. His Leadership Type needs to reach an agreement, decision, plan, or recommendation. Because his Type is solely focused on getting to a decision, 4th Basers might neglect taking time to listen and gather all the facts and information, reactions, or options before making a decision.

Dave Decider: "We're here to decide budget reductions for this year. To get us grounded, I'm going to share a few updates on our budget process and walk you through the document I have prepared for you today that outlines our list of reductions. Before I bring them to the board to be finalized, I wanted to share them with you. If we just extend our walking distance to our schools, we will save approximately $100,000. That would leave just $400,000 left to cut. Then, if we raised class sizes at the elementary and secondary schools, we could eliminate five teachers and get close to our goal."

Ian Information: "I think we need to hit pause, Dave. I sent detailed budget information to everyone before the meeting. I'd like to walk us through those details."

Rita Reactions: "Dave, I think you're jumping the gun. Our teachers will come unglued if they are the only ones to lose. We haven't even surveyed our staff to ask what reductions that they might recommend this year."

Dave Decider: "Rita, this is the most logical reduction to make and not everyone will like it. I've thought about this long and hard, and this is a good direction for our district."

Olivia Options: "There have to be other ideas we could consider that we haven't thought of yet. Maybe we could spread the cuts out among all staff in the district. Or increase revenue. We could ask voters for a tax increase."

Dave Decider: "Olivia, we could spend months thinking of all the options, but time is short. We need a decision."

Ian Information: "I can't help but think we need to get grounded as a team on key information in our budget. If we're going to support you, Dave, in bringing a recommendation forward to the board, we need to take the team through the revenue and expenditure reports for this year, the current budget projections for the upcoming year, and all the budget assumptions still relatively unknown. This team deserves to know what the budget recommendations are built on. This might take us an hour, but it would be time well spent."

Dave Decider: "Thank you for your feedback, Ian, but we don't have time for that type of process. We need to deliver a decision to the board, and there's no time like the present. Okay, everybody, let's decide. Are you in agreement with my plan to reduce $500,000 from our budget?"

Rita Reactions: "There's got to be a better way. Everyone is going to get super upset if we just go this direction."

Dave Decider: "That might be true, Rita, but we can't let emotion factor into what's clearly the correct decision."

Olivia Options: "I think we should take time and list all of the options we could cut out of our budget. By examining all the possibilities, we might see ideas we haven't considered."

Dave Decider: "Sorry, Olivia, we need a decision, and the one before us fits the needs. I have another meeting starting and I need to leave. I'm frustrated that we couldn't agree today on my recommendation, which is clearly a good decision for the budget reduction."

Dave leaves. The other team members are visibly shaken. Ian Info walks out with his remaining teammates.

Ian Information: "We're going to make a lousy decision if we don't get grounded on the full budget data ourselves."

Olivia Options: "I hope that the next meeting allows for the team to brainstorm a list of ideas, options, and possibilities for future potential reductions."

Rita Reactions: "I'm completely disappointed. The staff is going to lose it if they don't get a voice in this process. I can guarantee that. They're still upset about the last time this happened and they were left out."

More delays and discontent with the process. Yet another strikeout!

	IROD Chapter Review Questions
I	What are your key takeaways from this chapter?
R	What reactions do you have to the information shared in this chapter?
O	How did this chapter's ideas offer ways to enhance your decision-making process?
D	What ideas from this chapter could you apply immediately to your team's decision-making?

For bonus video clips, go to **HomerunLeadership.com/Bonus**

CHAPTER 12

Homerun Leadership Types Scenarios—The Homerun!

In great teams, conflict becomes productive. The free flow of conflicting ideas is critical for creative thinking, for discovering new solutions no one individual would have come to on his own.

PETER SENGE

Let's see the budget-reduction meeting one more time, in this instance with a leader using the best of Homerun Leadership to run the bases. You'll see a leader employ IROD to meet the needs of each Homerun Leadership Type to reach a great decision.

Ian Information will again take the lead, but he uses IROD to support each of the four Leadership Types, showing that he values priorities in the decision-making process and proving their importance in resolving team problems and reaching agreements.

Team Decision-making Leadership Type is focused on facts and details. True to his Type, Ian has already sent detailed budget documents for the team to review. He has also been recently trained on Homerun Leadership.

Watch as Ian leads.

Ian Information: "I know you've all been thinking hard about news from the board. We're here today to decide budget reductions for this year. To get us grounded, I'm going to highlight the process we'll use to determine our budget recommendations for the coming school year. We'll be taking time to ensure each of the four bases of decision-making is honored. I have four key questions to ensure each team Leadership Type is heard and supported today, and I've allotted time for us to gather any additional information, feedback, and ideas to assist us in reaching our decision."

"So here are the four questions that we will be using today. Each question will support the four decision-making leadership Types on teams, and this will follow the best science behind the four steps of decision-making and problem-solving. So here are our questions for today's meeting:"

- ◆ **1st Base—Information:** Can we gather all the information and data regarding this problem?
- ◆ **2nd Base—Reactions:** Can we gather all your reactions to the information we have gathered and shared?
- ◆ **3rd Base—Options:** Can we gather and list all the brainstormed options and ideas to address this problem and examine the pros and cons of each option?
- ◆ **4th Base—Decision:** What is the will of the team?

"As we complete the task at the 1st Base, we can move onto the next one. As we meet the requirements of each base, we'll also ask a wrap-up question for that base—'Anything else?' before we proceed to the next base."

"If I ask this wrap-up question and hear nothing—meaning no additional feedback—we'll move to the next base. If we get a response, I'll ask 'Anything else?' until we don't get any additional feedback. At that point, we can move onto the next base."

Ian continues, being careful to set up the IROD process and prepare the team for success.

Ian Information: "Prior to our meeting, I sent out budget documents and a video overview highlighting impact on our district. So now I'll ask our 1st Base IROD question: Can we gather all of the information we might need to make a decision on the problem we face of reducing $500,000 from our budget for the coming school year?"

"In my email and video overview, I asked for any questions or concerns you had about the budget, so we could maximize time budget-reduction options today. Is there any additional information you might need?"

Ian Information takes time to highlight the title of each budget document he prepared. For each document, he asks again if the team has questions or needs more information. Finally he asks if anyone has any remaining budget questions.

Ian Information: "Anything else?"

Team members have several clarifying questions. And when Ian asks "Anything else?" and no one has further queries, the team moves to the next base, gathering all the team feedback to information they know.

Ian Information: "I'm going to ask the 2nd Base question to gather reactions and feedback from our team to the budget data and information: 'Can we gather all of your reactions to the information we have provided, gathered, and shared?'"

Rita Reactions: "I'm concerned we haven't surveyed the staff to ask what reductions they might recommend this year. Could we do this?"

Ian Information: "Let's keep this idea on the board. You are suggesting a new decision, so let's see if we need to come back and make that decision once we have a team decision on budget reductions. Then we can make a determination on whether we should survey our staff to get their input."

Rita is pleased the team will consider her request for additional input.

Ian Information: "Are there any other reactions to the information we reviewed today? Anything else?"

Nobody responds, so Ian moves the team to the next base. The 3rd Base focuses on brainstorming options and possibilities.

Ian Information: "Our next problem-solving question is, 'Can we list all the brainstormed options and ideas to help us reduce our budget?' We'll start by adding Rita's idea to the list regarding a staff survey for more input."

Dave Decider: "If we just extend our walking distance to our schools, we could reduce our need for buses and that would save us approximately $100,000 in transportation expenses. That would leave us just $400,000 left to cut."

Olivia Options: "Thanks, Dave. Ian, I'd be happy to be the scribe and record ideas on the board for us. I'll put Dave's transportation-reduction idea first on our list."

Ian Information: "Who has other ideas to help us reach our goal?"

Dave Decider: "If we just raise class sizes at the elementary and secondary schools, we could eliminate five teachers and get close to our goal."

Olivia adds this idea to her list of brainstorms.

Olivia Options: "There must be other ideas we could consider. I'll share one I've been thinking about. I wonder if we could spread the cuts out among all staff in the district. I'm going to add my own idea to the list. I'll also add my idea that instead of cutting our budgets, maybe we could increase our revenue by asking voters for a tax increase."

Ian Information: "Thanks for that idea, Olivia. One point to consider: Even if we went out to the community for a tax-levy referendum, the dollars wouldn't arrive in the district until the following year, so we would still need to reduce our budgets for this year by $500,000. Oops—I'm jumping ahead to narrowing the list of options. I should have waited on that comment until our next base. I'll try to just brainstorm new ideas with the rest of you and keep capturing your ideas on the board, to keep the process moving forward."

The team appreciates Ian's recognition of his own mistake.

Dave Decider: "I think we could add another idea to the list. We could reduce the number of our classroom assistants and not reduce as many teachers. This would spread the cuts out more evenly around the district, and not just teachers would be impacted."

Ian Information: "Anything else, team? Now that I'm brainstorming myself, I think we could also spread the reductions more evenly, by including director departmental reductions to this list, to include reductions coming from every area of the district."

Rita Reactions: "Wow! That would greatly lessen the negative impact on just one or two areas, and reduce the negative feedback from our staff. If we are only reducing our budget by this lesser amount, we probably wouldn't need my survey idea to go out. We probably could decide this ourselves and not get much negative feedback due to the lessened impact."

Ian asks Olivia to read the list of ideas to this point, and she does.

Ian Information: "Can we discuss the pros/cons of each idea to help us narrow the list and find the ideas we most support reducing?"

The team agrees. The results of their discussion are this:

1. Increase the walking distance for students walking to school to reduce bus costs (estimated at $100,000).
   - **Pros:** It saves the district money.
   - **Cons:** Families hate it. Because children must walk significantly farther to school each morning, many families are forced to drive them.

2. Raise class size and only reduce classroom teachers (estimated $400,000 reduction).
   - **Pros:** It has a large impact on helping us meet our budget target.

♦ **Cons:** Teachers will face higher student counts in their room and not feel supported by being the only group that faces reductions.

3. Raise class size by reducing a combination of classroom teachers and classroom assistants (estimated $400,000 = $250,000 in teachers and $150,000 in classroom assistants).
   ♦ **Pros:** Reductions are spread across a couple of employee groups.
   ♦ **Cons:** Some classroom assistants will also need to be reduced which will decrease classroom support.

4. Spread the percentage of reduction equally across remaining areas. Assign a percentage cut to each administrative area not yet listed for reductions, and empower them to decide where to cut (estimated $100,000 as the target).
   ♦ **Pros:** Allows cuts to be more balanced by including all departments.
   ♦ **Cons:** Some areas may get undesirable reductions.

After discussing the pros and cons of each option, Ian asks the wrap-up question for 3rd Base.

Ian Information: "Are there any additional brainstormed ideas we can add to the list? Anything else?"

Following good teaching practice, Ian waits ten seconds to ensure no one has another idea. After this "wait time," he continues.

Ian Information: "Hearing none, can we each place a dot by our top two choices for reductions based on the list of pros/cons?"

The team places dots indicating their choices.

Ian Information: "Well it looks like taking $400,000 by reducing both teachers and classroom assistants was our top vote getter, and taking $100,000 in the administrative department from areas not yet reduced received the second-most votes. This looks like we potentially have reached our goal. If the team can support these top two items, we can bring these recommendations to the school board for their approval, as well. Before we vote, are there any questions or concerns from the team?

The team is silent until Rita Reactions jumps in.

Rita Reactions: "Well, as painful as budget reductions are, it seems like we made the most equitable and fair decision today."

Ian Information: "This was a true team effort today. I really appreciate each of your voices and support to get us across the finish line together. In any case, do we have the will of the group to support this? Please show me a thumbs up if you support this, and a thumbs down if you cannot get behind this. Can everyone stand with this? Do we have the will of the team?"

Dave Decider: "I can. My thumb is up, and I have another meeting starting. I'm sorry, but I have to leave."

Ian calls on the one team member who hasn't responded.

Olivia Options: "Yes."

Ian Information: "And I'm a yes. I think we have an agreement to take to the board next week. Have a good meeting, Dave. Thanks to everyone. I will get this typed up and sent to the board for approval."

IROD Frameworks

That's a great decision supported by each team member—and fulfilling to all four Leadership Types. That's a Homerun!

Before we move on, let me introduce this discussion in a format I call an "IROD Framework." I'll share more frameworks in chapter 14 and more at the end of the book.

IROD Frameworks are useful as a starting point for your team decision, reminding you of the questions to ask as you run the bases. Filled in with the details of a discussion, they allow you to quickly overview and critique your adherence to the IROD process.

TEAM IROD: Reduce Annual Budget by $500,000		
I	**Do we have all the INFORMATION on this topic?** Can we and have we gathered all the information we might need to make a decision on the problem we face of reducing $500,000 from our budget for the coming school year? Does anyone have any budget questions? Do you need any additional reports or information? **TEAM INFORMATION:** • We need to reduce the budget by $500,000 • We have all the budget reports and enrollment trends for the school district	**Anything else?**
R	**Do we have everyone's REACTIONS to the information?** Can we gather all your reactions to the information we have provided, gathered and shared? **TEAM REACTIONS:** • I'm concerned that we haven't surveyed the staff to ask what reductions they might recommend this year. Could we do this?	**Anything else?** Budget reductions are the worst.

Have we brainstormed all OPTIONS, listed pros and cons for each, and prioritized the list? Can we list all the brainstormed options and ideas to help us reduce our budget?				Anything else?
Team's Brainstormed OPTIONS	PROS	CONS	Reprioritized Options List	
1. Extend walking distance	◆ Helps reduce budget by about $100,000	◆ Parents get upset	**Homerun Balanced Budget Reduction Recommendations:**	
2. Raise class sizes and only reduce classroom teachers	◆ Helps reduce budget	◆ Teachers and parents get upset ◆ Proven that larger class sizes leads to increased discipline issues and learning gaps	**a.** Reduce Paraprofessionals -$150,000 **b.** Raise class sizes (to reduce teachers) - $250,000	
3. Raise class size by reducing a combination of classroom teachers and classroom assistants	◆ Helps reduce overall budget in a balanced approach	◆ Reduces support for students and teachers in the classrooms	**c.** Reduce administrative budgets - $100,000 Reduction Total: $500,000	
4. Spread reductions equally to all areas, like directors, so every department faces reductions	◆ Helps to better meet the budget-reduction target ◆ Cuts are spread out	◆ No director wants to reduce their budget		

	Is the DECISION the will of the group? Can everyone support this? Do we have the will of the team?	Anything else?
D	**OUR DECISION:** Our entire team voted to support this plan. No one is happy (because it's still a budget reduction), but we are pleased to have an agreement.	Well, as painful as budget reductions are, it seems like we made the most equitable and fair decision today.

	IROD Chapter Review Questions
I	What are your key takeaways from this chapter?
R	What reactions do you have to the information shared in this chapter?
O	How did this chapter's ideas offer ways to enhance your decision-making process?
D	What ideas from this chapter could you apply immediately to your team's decision-making?

For bonus video clips, go to **HomerunLeadership.com/Bonus**

CHAPTER 13

Leadership Types Playing Together

What makes you different or weird, that's your strength.

MERYL STREEP

In the span of an hour-and-a-half team meeting, Ian Information moved from Regular Leadership to Homerun Leadership.

You too can make that same powerful shift.

Even if you aren't the person in charge—and perhaps your team hasn't been trained in IROD—you're capable of helping every meeting or decision scenario run more smoothly and conclude in success.

Each of us has all the potential to be a great leader if we support everyone on our team by learning about the four Homerun Leadership Types, understanding the order of the IROD bases and the Homerun Basepath, and learning to ask the four Homerun Leadership Questions (and the clean-up question).

In every decision-making situation, effective teams take a few extra minutes to touch all the bases:

◆ The 1st Baser needs information (check!).

◆ The 2nd Baser wants everyone to have the opportunity to voice their reactions (check!).

◆ The 3rd Baser highly values listing all possible options and discussing insights and objections as a team (check!).

◆ The 4th Baser wants to cross options off the list, narrowing the list and narrowing some more, until the will of the group is clear and a decision made (check!).

Consider my camp director story. When things turned difficult and decisions needed to be made, I went directly to my 4th Base Leadership tactic of "pushership." I was the great decider who told everyone what to do, rather than taking into consideration the other three Leadership Types.

"All those who disagree with me, please raise your hands and say 'I resign.'"

As Dave Decider, I ended up telling people what to do instead of getting all the INFORMATION from 1st Base Leadership Types, hearing the REACTIONS of 2nd Base Leadership Types, and listening to OPTIONS of 3rd Base Leadership Types.

As leader, I repeatedly failed to take the time to secure the support of my team. If I had just known how to run the bases—and had committed to work closely with other Leadership Types—I would have reached a shared team decision and avoided all the resistance and stress I caused.

This is why it's so critical to learn HOW to support all four Leadership Types and the order of WHEN to include each Types. And IROD shows us the repeatable, science-based path.

Now, I understand what makes a great team. It's people of varying Homerun Leadership Types making a habit of using IROD to contribute their best to make great team decisions. By rounding the bases together, we make collaborative choices everyone can support.

That's a true team effort.

Is it always that easy?

Absolutely not.

It all sounds nice, but there's a small problem with that ideal. Few of us are ever taught HOW to do that.

Under pressure, we each tend to fall back on our strongest leadership skill, because that's where we're most comfortable. In that scenario, our dominant Leadership Type can quickly create disastrous team moments.

Why? When our top leadership skill takes over, we often forget to support the needs of the other three Leadership Types.

**Team members become frustrated when leaders
don't meet their needs or use their gifts.**

The result is poorer-quality decisions not supported by—or benefitting from—the Homerun Leadership gifts of the whole team.

The solution is always the same. Ask the Homerun Leadership questions. Stick to IROD. Run the basepath every time!

	IROD Chapter Review Questions
I	What are your key takeaways from this chapter?
R	What reactions do you have to the information shared in this chapter?
O	How did this chapter's ideas offer ways to enhance your decision-making process?
D	What ideas from this chapter could you apply immediately to your team's decision-making?

For bonus video clips, go to **HomerunLeadership.com/Bonus**

CHAPTER 14

Running the Bases Every Time

Great decision-making comes from the ability to create the time and space to think rationally and intelligently about the issue at hand.

GRAHAM ALLCOT

IROD works because it makes explicit a thought process that happens instinctively. In many situations, we reach decisions almost instantly, without a pause to examine our reasoning!

This rapid-fire internal process works well for individual decisions. But it creates difficulties as soon as others are impacted by a choice. Partners sense tension. Teams feel frustrated when points in the decision-making process are left unstated and undebated—watch out!

Regular Leaders skip over IROD steps based on the preferences of whoever controls the decision-making process.

Homerun Leaders run the Homerun Basepath. Every time.

To get further practice in IROD and increase your success average, let's look at a few decision-making situations. We'll see how the IROD steps look in three everyday settings—as an individual, in one-on-one partner situations, and with a team. We'll put them in slow motion so we can observe and consciously replicate the process. We'll wrap up with that instant-replay view of a high stakes work situation, our budget reduction process.

These practice scenarios offer practical insights you can use right away.

This homerun batting practice will prepare you to handle all sizes and shapes of struggles—always starting with the Homerun questions. If you forget everything else—easy to do, especially under stress—just ask those IROD questions.

- When you face an individual challenge or struggle, if you ask these questions to yourself, you will start hitting more personal Homeruns immediately.
- If you ask IROD questions with yourself and another individual, you will hit more partner Homeruns and make both of you much happier.
- And if you ask these questions with your team, MAKING SURE YOU DON'T SKIP BASES, you'll hit way more team Homeruns. It's like hitting a grand slam. When my team is happy because we made a great team decision, I'm happy!

Running the bases every time means always asking those four Homerun questions. Each of them. In the correct order. Without exception.

REMINDER: Have one more look at the IROD Homerun questions. Then close your eyes. Can you say them verbatim? Make sure you have these memorized so you're ready for your next decision-making situation— whether individual, between you and a partner, or with a team.

IROD Homerun Questions	
QUESTION	CLEANUP QUESTION
Do we have all the INFORMATION on this topic?	Anything else?
Do we have everyone's REACTIONS to the information?	Anything else?
Have we brainstormed all the OPTIONS, listed pros and cons of each, and prioritized the list?	Anything else?
Is the DECISION the will of the group?	Anything else?

3rd BASE DETAIL: Before we move to practice, I want to share one last piece of coaching, this time more specifically about 3rd Base. At 3rd Base, there is one question, but it has three steps. Here's the question again:

Have we brainstormed all the OPTIONS, listed pros and cons of each, and prioritized the list?

As you work with your team to answer this question, you need to:

1. List all the brainstormed options (on a whiteboard, on a shared Google Doc, etc.).
2. List all the pros and cons of each option.
3. Reprioritize the list based on the pros and cons.

If you can master 3rd Base by slowing down and completing these three steps, you can dramatically increase your Leadership Batting Average and hit more homeruns.

Run the Bases: Individual Example

Can you use the four IROD questions to fix your own problem? Absolutely. In my case, a few good questions saved a few thousand dollars.

A few years ago, we were trying to refinance our house. When we received our appraisal in the mail from the appraisal company, our home value came back much lower than I had expected. I was frustrated because I wanted to refinance and take cash out to pay off my kids' college loans.

I wasn't sure what to do next, so I decided to take my own medicine. I forced myself to run the bases, asking and answering the four Homerun Leadership questions. Here's my thought process:

INDIVIDUAL IROD: Can I fix my own problem?		
Do we have all the INFORMATION on this topic? What do I see on this appraisal? Does anything look unexpected? Is this appraisal value enough for my objective? **DAVE'S INFORMATION:** • I spent $600 on an appraisal. • When I reviewed the results, my home appraisal seemed much lower than it should be. • The comparables they used for my house don't seem like good comparables. • Lake property is often hard to find good comparables for because people rarely sell their lake homes.	**I**	**Anything else?**
Do we have everyone's REACTIONS to the information? How do I feel about the information I just learned on this appraisal? **DAVE'S REACTIONS:** • I'm really upset that the comparables the appraisal company used have negatively impacted my appraisal value. • This bad appraisal will negatively impact my future financial picture!	**R**	**Anything else?** *I feel like I got the shaft here.*

	Have we brainstormed all OPTIONS, listed pros and cons for each, and prioritized the list? Is there anything I can do about this bad appraisal? Do I have any recourse?			Anything else?
	Team's Brainstormed OPTIONS	**PROS**	**CONS**	**Reprioritized Options List**
O	**1.** COMPLAIN: I could complain a lot and hope my future would change.	♦ Complaining may make me feel better.	♦ Complaining won't fix this problem.	**1.** CALL **2.** COMPLAIN **3.** NOTHING **4.** YELL
	2. CALL: I could call the company and ask for a new appraisal.	♦ Calling the company may result in a new, correct appraisal that could positively change my financial future.	♦ I'm a little reluctant and embarrassed to call the company to question their work.	
	3. YELL: I could yell and be upset with the world.	♦ Yelling might make me feel better.	♦ Yelling won't change the valuation of my house appraisal.	
	4. NOTHING: I could do nothing and move on.	♦ Less work	♦ More pain and agony	
D	**Is the DECISION the will of the group?** Well, what am I going to do? **DAVE'S DECISION:** Since there's only one good clear option, I DECIDE to prepare for this big phone call.			Anything else?

To get ready for the call, I drive to each of the three houses the appraiser used to value my house and check to see if they indeed were good comparables, gathering more INFORMATION for the call I need to make. As I collect more information on these appraisals, I get even more upset—my REACTION. It gave me the energy and detail I needed to get up the courage to call.

When I act on my DECISION and call, the company agrees to a new appraisal, and my new evaluation comes back $135,000 higher the second time around.

Huge HOMERUN! Go IROD!

Run the Bases: Partner Example

I rarely cook dinner, but I coordinate what we eat every night. Some nights are easier than others, but I always look for a Homerun agreement.

Most nights when I leave work, I call home to discuss dinner with my wife. Typically we're both hungry, but I check to make sure she hasn't eaten a late lunch or made last-minute plans. Once I've cleared that basic INFORMATION, I remind her that it's Friday, so we had planned to have pizza. I like that idea, but she immediately groans and says, "I am so sick of pizza!" We have arrived at REACTIONS. Well, that's okay. I'm flexible. Pizza sounds delicious, but if she's burned out on one of our favorites, I can always swing by a pizza place at lunch tomorrow. No big deal. On to our OPTIONS.

PARTNER IROD: What's for Dinner?		
Do we have all the INFORMATION on this topic? What's in the refrigerator that we could eat for dinner? What did we both eat for lunch? **DAVE'S INFORMATION:** • We typically do pizza on Fridays to get the weekend started. • But I'm also flexible, including stopping and picking up something quick from the grocery store or a drive-through, just so long as dinner isn't at midnight. **PARTNER INFORMATION:** • She offers to make hamburgers, which are currently frozen. • She's burned out on pizza.	**Anything else?** It's already 5:30.	I
Do we have everyone's REACTIONS to the information? What are your reactions to what is in the refrigerator? Do we eliminate what we ate for lunch from our list of options? **DAVE'S REACTIONS:** • I still love pizza. I could eat pizza every day. • I'm not willing to wait a long time for dinner to be ready. **PARTNER INFORMATION:** • She's sick of pizza, but willing to start working on whatever we have at home, which isn't much.	**Anything else?** I'm already starving!	R

	Have we brainstormed all OPTIONS, listed pros and cons for each, and prioritized the list? What ideas can you brainstorm as dinner options to eat tonight and what are the pros and cons of each option?				Anything else?
O	**Our Brainstormed OPTIONS**	**PROS**	**CONS**	**Reprioritized Options List**	
	1. PIZZA	♦ I love pizza.	♦ She is hating the idea of pizza.	1. CHICKEN 2. HAM-BURGERS 3. PIZZA	
	2. CHICKEN	♦ This is the healthiest and quickest option.	♦ I have to stop at the store.		
	3. HAM-BURGER	♦ This option sounds good.	♦ The hamburger is frozen and will take way too long to cook.		
D	**Is the DECISION the will of the group?** Of the ideas we brainstormed, what was your top choice to eat for dinner tonight? **DAVE'S DECISION:** We decided on chicken tonight. I am going to stop and pick this up on my way home.				Anything else?

Now it's clear that we're both hungry, but the original plan is a bust. It's time to move on to brainstorming some new OPTIONS.

1. My wife says we have a pound of hamburger in the freezer she's been planning to make into burgers. It's frozen solid, however, so dinner would be late .

2. I offer to stop and pick up a rotisserie chicken and some rolls. Definitely a contender!

3. I had pizza as a previous option, but that's eliminated based on her reaction. But it's still an option for tomorrow!

We quickly rule out hamburgers because we're both too hungry to wait that long. But burgers make it onto the plan for tomorrow, when she can start early on supper. Between rotisserie chicken and pizza, we're both enthusiastic about chicken—our DECISION.

We're happy and well fed. HOMERUN!

Run the Bases: Team Example

It's Saturday night, and my daughter says, "Dad, I'm taking the car tonight." Immediately, two of our other kids speak up with reasons why that won't work. They too have plans that involve the car.

Team IROD: I'm taking the car tonight	
Do we have all the INFORMATION on this topic? What does everyone have going on tonight? How many cars do we have in the household? What time are the events, and which plans require the car? **TEAM INFORMATION:** • B has a baseball game at 6:00. • M has a drive-in movie; wants to get there by 7:00 for tailgating. • Dad has to go grocery shopping and hit the gym. • There's only one car available tonight.	**Anything else?** It's 3:00 now.
Do we have everyone's REACTIONS to the information? How do we feel about the information we just learned? **TEAM REACTIONS:** • Nearly in unison, everyone says "You can't take the car tonight!" • M says, "I HAVE to take the car. I already told all my friends that would pick them up!" • B says, "I HAVE to get to my game!!" • Mom says, "I'm taking my car to my book club. Dad, can you figure this out? I'm outta here." • Dad says, "I gotta get groceries or you're all going to starve, but I don't mind having a reason to skip the gym."	**Anything else?** Do we need to have a schedule for the car?

Have we brainstormed all OPTIONS, listed pros and cons for each, and prioritized the list? Is there a way to get everyone's needs met?			Anything else?
Team's Brainstormed OPTIONS	**PROS**	**CONS**	**Reprioritized Options List**
1. FIGHT	◆ You get to keep arguing.	◆ Fighting won't fix this problem ◆ Could result in everyone's plans getting canceled.	1. COORDI-NATE A WIN 2. ROCK, PAPER, SCISSORS 3. PARENTAL VETO 4. FIGHT
2. ROCK, PAPER, SCISSORS	◆ Someone will win	◆ Only one winner	
3. PARENTAL VETO	◆ Dad might choose one of the kids' plans ◆ Groceries will get bought - no one will starve	◆ All kids could lose	
4. COORDI-NATE A WIN	◆ Possibility for everyone to win by developing a plan to maximize limited resources (i.e., the car)	◆ We have to spend 10-15 minutes working this out.	

	Is the DECISION the will of the group? Can we all agree to make this plan work?	Anything else?
D	**OUR DECISION:** We can make this all work if Dad hustles to the gym and store and gets back in time for M to drop B off at baseball. M will then keep the car through the evening, and B is responsible for getting a ride home with a friend, or worst case, an Uber.	Dad, get to the store right NOW. Go.

Whatever the circumstances you face and the decision at hand, when you use four IROD Homerun Questions to run the bases, you'll cross home plate, together.

If you've made it to the end of this chapter, I want to reward you with one more Homerun Framework. Here is my favorite go-to framework when a system, program, or even your own team needs improvement.

Your team likely needs to run an annual process to improve a system or program. In my world, that's high school commencement, a huge community and school district event. The day after the ceremony, we always spend an hour with the following framework to improve next year's event. Here's a great set of questions to drive innovation and improvement.

		TEAM INNOVATION AND IMPROVEMENT	
		Use these questions to guide an improvement conversation with your team.	
I	1st	Can we each share what is working well with our current plan?	Anything else?
R	2nd	Can we each share what isn't working as well as it could be?	Anything else?
O	3rd	Can we brainstorm a list of options and ideas to improve what isn't working as well as it could be, list pros and cons for each and prioritize the list?	Anything else?
D	4th	Of the ideas we brainstormed, can we agree as a majority with our reprioritized list of improvements?	Anything else?

As a leader, you can practice IROD at every turn of life. But let's look more at best practices for running the bases with your team.

	IROD Chapter Review Questions
I	What are your key takeaways from this chapter?
R	What reactions do you have to the information shared in this chapter?
O	How did this chapter's ideas offer ways to enhance your decision-making process?
D	What ideas from this chapter could you apply immediately to your team's decision making?

For bonus video clips, go to **HomerunLeadership.com/Bonus**

CHAPTER 15

Slow Down to Go Fast

If you want to go fast, go alone,
if you want to go far, go together.

AFRICAN PROVERB

High-performing Homerun Leadership teams are notable for their success at reaching agreement on plans and decisions. It's their not-so-secret power to take the best next steps to reach their goals. Together!

If teams commit to doing the work, knowing the bases, and following them in order, they INEVITABLY undergo a transformation. They PREDICTABLY become high-performing. If they let themselves fall into old habits, they will stay a regular team that struggles with resistance, frustration, and low performance.

High-performing teams build and maintain their high performance by consistently, constantly, and continually using good process, facilitation, and collaboration.

So why do leaders and teams stick with Regular Leadership when Homerun Leadership is available to them?

**Homerun Leadership is simple to understand and
easy to implement. But at first, it feels counterintuitive.**

Let's be honest about human nature and the impulses all leaders feel. When things heat up, your natural instincts will be to shut down input.

Every bone in your body will resist the IROD process.

When leadership stress rises—and, at some point, it does for everyone— our tendencies tell us,

> **Shut it down.**
> **Just decide.**
> **Fast.**
> **Problem solved!**

Except. Over my many years in leadership, my worst decisions are the ones I made quickly, alone, and without input and discussion. Remember, your intuition as a Regular Leader will tell you to go faster. To shortcut process. To resolve an issue as quickly as possible.

Homerun Leadership tells you to slow down, follow the process, touch every base, and find team agreement. The counterintuitive aspect is this: By slowing down and following the process, you arrive at the best team decision faster. Why? Because you get to this optimum decision on the first try rather than spending hours and hours revisiting the subject.

**Skipping a base means you'll come back to your decision over
and over.**

What happens if your team misses a base? It's completely predictable:

	What happens if your team misses a base?
I	If you miss gathering all the INFORMATION, decisions will be based on partial information and emotions will increase during your decision-making process. Your team will have a difficult time making a good decision.
R	If you miss gathering all the participants' REACTIONS to the information, they won't make a personal connection to the situation. They will engage more as bystanders rather than as vested problem-solvers.
O	If you miss gathering all possible OPTIONS or forget to examine the pros and cons of choices, teams will miss the opportunity to push thinking and make the best possible decision.
D	If you miss reaching a team DECISION, your team will become frustrated that your process is stalled or spinning.

(Hanson, 2005)

When it feels like the IROD process will take too long, remember that because you are focused on which base you're on and the task to be accomplished at each base, you'll be able to continuously move forward. Be thorough, organized, and transparent. And you'll now be leading with the wind at your back.

There are obvious signs your team is missing bases. Be aware of these any of these alerts:

1. You make people mad!
2. People want to just push through (to make a decision or meet a deadline).
3. Conversations are coerced instead of inviting and warm.
4. You regularly delay decisions for future meetings because you can't reach team agreement.
5. You hear team frustration rising.
6. You see anger.
7. Members search for a new leader.

8. Members opt off the team, costing their organization time and money.
9. Teams don't reach goals.
10. Teams make decisions based on flawed or partial data.
11. Teams don't gather feedback from the team or other stakeholders.
12. Decisions are made by individuals instead of whole teams.
13. Decisions are dictated by power rather than created through collaboration.
14. Teams miss options and need to revisit their decisions.
15. Team members feel like meetings are a waste of time.
16. Impromptu meetings after the meetings are where team members voice their real opinions.
17. Decisions get made before or after meetings.
18. People don't feel heard.
19. Participants grandstand rather than engage in dialogue.
20. You feel resistance.
21. You know you're making decisions not supported by your team.
22. Team trust decreases.
23. Team dysfunction increases.
24. Leaders who consistently fail to run the bases fail to keep their jobs.

There indeed is one accelerator that won't shortcut the process. Gather and disseminate as much IROD data as possible ahead of time. That might mean tasking individuals to provide reports or meeting with subgroups of your team in advance. At your decision-making team meeting, you will still need to recap the Information, Reactions, and Options—and allow for team discussion at each base—but this prework will accelerate team discussions because much of the content is no longer new.

When I enter a team meeting, I always believe I'm not walking in with the best ideas. My goal is not only to bring my ideas to the team but also to bring an open mind to listen to, hear, and weigh the merit of every idea from the team. The goal of every meeting is to leave the room with the best idea, the choice that has the buy-in of a majority of the team.

To help yourself, you have to help others. If you want to win, you need to help others win. If you want a Homerun, you must touch every base. The goal is to meet everyone's needs on your way to the best decision.

The more you practice these strategies by running the bases daily, the more natural this process will feel.

	IROD Chapter Review Questions
I	What are your key takeaways from this chapter?
R	What reactions do you have to the information shared in this chapter?
O	How did this chapter's ideas offer ways to enhance your decision-making process?
D	What ideas from this chapter could you apply immediately to your team's decision-making?

For bonus video clips, go to **HomerunLeadership.com/Bonus**

CHAPTER 16

Slow Down to Go Long

A genuine leader is not a searcher for consensus but a molder of consensus.

MARTIN LUTHER KING JR.

There are many daily situations in which running the bases can result in a quick resolution. Going slow to go fast ensures you make the best team decision the first time and reduce your need to backtrack.

That said, IROD is also your process of choice for long-haul decisions that will NEVER resolve quickly—nor should they!

There are times when managing the IROD process takes weeks, months, or even years to complete.

I call these situations "Long Homeruns."

For example, in my school district, a large facility project—with a request for community funding—often takes between one to two years to complete. In our past construction bond request for our community, we had to thoroughly study each site, determine the greatest needs for each site, and prioritize those needs.

With large construction projects, several task forces were set up as well to develop key program areas to best utilize the future construction enhancements. Our early learning taskforce, for example, focused on best practices and placement in our district for early-learning programs. Each decision took months to fully run the bases of a good IROD process, and ultimately made for a fantastic overall composite construction request for our community.

In the end, after many small IROD decisions were packaged into one community yes-or-no vote, we made our pitch to the community, and the bond-referendum vote passed.

Can you picture that—and similar situations in your own sphere of decision-making? It was one heck of a huge Homerun with nearly two years' worth of significant Homerun-team decisions along the way. I can't think of a better way to describe the process and all the work it entails than the "Long Homerun."

	IROD Chapter Review Questions
I	What are your key takeaways from this chapter?
R	What reactions do you have to the information shared in this chapter?
O	How did this chapter's ideas offer ways to enhance your decision-making process?
D	What ideas from this chapter could you apply immediately to your team's decision-making?

For bonus video clips, go to **HomerunLeadership.com/Bonus**

CHAPTER 17

What Is "Homerun Consensus?"

*To Confucius, harmony was consensus, not conformity.
It required loyal opposition.*

EVAN OSNOS

Homeruns are about making decisions everyone on the team can support, no matter their starting point—their own Homerun Leadership Type.

But "approval" of a decision can be fuzzy. Who's happy with the choice? And precisely how happy are they?

The situation invites a question. In making the best team decisions possible, what is consensus? If your goal is to hit a Homerun, how do you know when you've crossed the plate together and notched a win for everyone?

When our leadership team gathers to make a decision, we first need a definition of consensus for the group. As our team discussed options to produce a "Homerun Consensus," we brainstormed several possibilities, such as:

1. 51%
2. 75%
3. 90%

In classic IROD fashion, we discussed and listed out the pros and cons of each option. The list then looked like this:

Percentage for Consensus	Pros of this Percentage	Cons of this Percentage
1. 51%	It's the majority.	It's not a strong majority.
2. 75%	It's a strong majority.	It may be hard to achieve 75%.
3. 90%	It's a super strong team majority.	It may be nearly impossible to reach and almost requires a unanimous vote to achieve this level of approval.

As our team members shared their perspectives, they seemed to be concerned about 51% harming the decision-making process for our team, and that bad decisions could actually get through our team process filter.

So that option was dropped lower on the list of possible options we could support.

Next, the option of 90% approval faced even stronger criticism, with all of us foreseeing the need for nearly unanimous support on any future item. Decisions were highly unlikely to get through this strong team filter.

This option ultimately ranked lowest on our list of desirable choices. With two options that had little support, the team quickly rallied around 75% as the approval rate for our definition of "team consensus." The agreement chart, with the highest-ranked option in the first position looks like this:

Percentage for Consensus	Pros of this Percentage	Cons of this Percentage	Actual Ranked Options
1. 51%	It's the majority.	It's not a strong majority.	1. 75% 2. 51% 3. 90%
2. 75%	It's a strong majority.	It may be hard to achieve 75%.	
3. 90%	It's a super strong team majority.	It may be nearly impossible to reach and almost requires a unanimous vote to achieve this level of approval.	

The Super Card

One final note. While our team always tries to make consensus decisions, there are times when I still need to make the decision alone.

As a group, we recognize that the IROD process has resulted in the best decisions for our school district. But our team also gives me the right to exercise my individual ability to make tough decisions, especially when team consensus isn't feasible. This "Super Card" (as in Superintendent) I can play at any time isn't taken lightly.

I try to not play this card unless it's truly necessary. Why? Whenever our team can share additional Information, Reactions, and Options and assist in prioritizing the Decision, it strengthens the outcome for our entire school community.

	IROD Chapter Review Questions
I	What are your key takeaways from this chapter?
R	What reactions do you have to the information shared in this chapter?
O	How did this chapter's ideas offer ways to enhance your decision-making process?
D	What ideas from this chapter could you apply immediately to your team's decision-making?

For bonus video clips, go to **HomerunLeadership.com/Bonus**

CHAPTER 18

Team Facilitation Tactics

The way a team plays as a whole determines its success. You may have the greatest bunch of individual stars in the world, but if they don't play together, the club won't be worth a dime.

BABE RUTH

Implementing Homerun Leadership with your team doesn't mean you throw out everything else you know about good facilitation. Don't lessen the power of the IROD Homerun questions with bad team leadership.

Keep these tips to keep in mind as you help your team move from point A to B.

Engage

1. **Remain neutral.** If you don't take sides during the decision-making process, you can better support the entire team.
2. **Be a good listener.** Capturing the whole story grounds you in all the Information and Reactions—spoken and below-the-surface—of a team problem. Real listening brings your team together and moves you forward together.

3. **Take notes.** Besides supporting the good listening quality of good facilitation, taking notes allows you to go back and get clarification on the problem if you miss any points.

4. **Create a safe place where all voices on the team are heard.** If you want the best decisions, hearing all voices will allow you to get all the Information, Reactions, Options, and the ultimate team Decision. Prompt people who aren't natural talkers to share.

5. **Establish team norms.** To ensure all perspectives are honored and supported during your team conversations, you will want to establish a few team norms as you begin your time together.

   ◆ Common team norms include (Karten, 2012):

      i Meetings will start on time.

      ii A pre-designated scribe will take minutes.

      iii A pre-designated facilitator will lead the meeting.

      iv An agenda will be published in advance.

      v Decision making is by consensus.

      vi Team members will hold themselves and each other accountable for commitments made to one another.

Use the IROD Vocabulary

   ◆ Tell people what you're doing. Informing your team about the what, how, and why of IROD will help them come along in a discussion that benefits everyone.

   ◆ Vocalize the IROD words and the bases to know where you are on the Homerun Basepath.

Always Run the Bases

- Ask IROD Homerun questions, keeping them in front of you as a checklist. If you can follow the science, you'll reach success.
- Memorize and practice the questions to build your confidence.
- You satisfy the needs of all Leadership Types by asking each of these questions. Every time!
- Remember: If you skip a base, you skip success.

Remember the Clean-Up Question: Anything Else?

- After asking each of the core IROD questions, ensure you've completely touched each base by asking "Anything else?"
- Keep asking this essential question until no one responds with further thoughts. "Crickets are your ticket" to move forward to the next base.

Go Back to Go Forward

- Ask the IROD questions in order—until you can't.
- If someone injects a new point—Information, Reaction, or Option—you can't keep pushing forward. Identify out loud which base you need to go back to, and ask the required questions to address this new thought.
- For example, if new information is presented, you'll need to go all the way back to 1st Base. If a new concern or reaction emerges, it's time to touch 2nd Base again. Sometimes people come in at the last minute with an option or idea that hasn't been considered. It might be the best one so far. Go back to 3rd Base and vet it!
- Once you've addressed the new point, you'll be able to move forward again.

When You're Stuck, Retrace Your Steps

- If you feel stuck and can't move forward, go backwards.
- Double-check that you've completed each Base by asking the appropriate IROD Question and Cleanup question to satisfy the needs of each type.
- If all else fails, restart at 1st Base, re-ask each IROD question, and you'll get new traction to keep moving.

Use IROD Visuals

- As you work with your team, make the Homerun Leadership Basepath visible. Your visual aid will 1) allow everyone to follow along as you run the bases together, 2) accelerate the team decision-making process as people remain connected to the process, and 3) show the path forward to a better, faster team decision.
- Setting up a solid visual structure also helps you to be a better facilitator. If you can lean on the visual tool wherever and whenever you're asked to guide a group, you'll more effectively move people from point A to B.
- Here are examples of formats I frequently use, depending on the situation:

1st	I
2nd	R
3rd	O
4th	D

This is the layout I use with my team and we're all viewing the same document, as in Google Docs.

OR

1st I	2nd R
3rd O	4th D

This format is useful when you are working off a piece of flipchart paper and have limited space. You may have this example hanging on the wall and use a piece of flip-chart paper to fill as you ask the 4 key questions.

OR

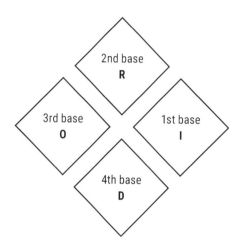

This is the Homerun Basepath visual that works so well in keeping participants informed where we are at in the process.

Put Options in the Open

◆ Making the list of 3rd Base Options visible is especially helpful as you begin to list and weigh the pros and cons of each brainstormed option.

◆ As you cross off Options that are no longer viable from your 3rd Base list, don't erase them! A future option may arise that was based on a previously discarded option, and it could end up becoming part of your final decision. Just put a line through the Option. Don't let it be forgotten.

Prioritize Options

- After you have listed pros and cons to all 3rd Base Options and only a couple of options remain, get clarity on team progress in the decision-making process.
- Go ahead and ask which way team members are leaning—to Option A or Option B. Their responses will give you a sense of where team members are at without asking for a final decision.
- This tactic allows team members to safely approach 4th Base—the actual decision—without feeling the pressure of officially deciding.
- You're allowing people to try on different solutions. It's just like trying on a piece of clothing and critiquing your reflection before making a purchase.
- You might discover immediately that the group already agrees on a single Option. In this case, you've quietly made your decision and you simply need to confirm, "Is this Decision the will of the group?" If the answer is yes, you have a HOMERUN!

Confirm and Offer Closure

- Give your team an opportunity to confirm they're on board with the final decision to ensure you've reached an agreement.
- Even as you move to a vote, provide space to ask the question "Anything else?"
- Allow discussion to restore possible hurt feelings from the journey that can be cleared up now.
- Ample time at the end of the process lets people remain involved and get fully behind an agreement, even if it wasn't their first choice.

Cross Home Plate Together

◆ It's also not a Homerun if I buy movie tickets for a movie for my family without first talking to them. It's only a Homerun when we cross home plate TOGETHER!

	IROD Chapter Review Questions
I	What are your key takeaways from this chapter?
R	What reactions do you have to the information shared in this chapter?
O	How did this chapter's ideas offer ways to enhance your decision-making process?
D	What ideas from this chapter could you apply immediately to your team's decision-making?

For bonus video clips, go to **HomerunLeadership.com/Bonus**

CHAPTER 19

Who Decides What— Governance or Management?

We cannot be mere consumers of good governance, we must be participants; we must be co-creators.

ROHINI NILEKANI

Within every organization, sooner or later questions arise about WHO gets to make decisions. Homerun Leadership doesn't dictate the answer. But it's indeed crucial for you to know which individual or group should run the Homerun Basepath for a specific decision. In a nutshell, your organization and any documents of incorporation define key roles and responsibilities. Combine that with good practice and other organizational tradition, and you can determine who decides what. It's all a question of Governance vs. Management.

In the nonprofit sector, for example, churches and school districts operate with governing boards. In the business world, so do larger companies.

In each organization, the governing board operates with a typical set of key responsibilities. The board is responsible for oversight and planning, while management executes daily operations. Each group has its own roles and should know the importance of maintaining clear lines of distinction. When board directors and managers stay in their lanes and stick to their responsibilities in decision-making, organizations run more smoothly (Eisenstein, 2021).

The following chart highlights key roles and responsibilities of Governance and Management (Bader, 2008):

The Board-Management Relationship

Board's Roles	Management's Roles
Select, evaluate, and support the CEO.	• Run the organization in line with board direction. • Keep the board educated and informed. • Seek the board's counsel.
Approve high-level organizational goals and policies.	• Recommend goals and policies, supported by background information.
Make major decisions.	• Frame decisions in the context of the mission and strategic vision and bring the board well-documented recommendations.
Oversee management and organizational performance.	• Bring the board timely information in concise, contextual, or comparative formats. • Communicate with candor and transparency. • Be responsive to requests for additional information.
Act as external advocates and diplomats in public policy, fundraising, and stakeholder/community relations.	Keep the board informed, bring recommendations, and mobilize directors to leverage their external connections to support the organization.

(Bader, 2008)

136

In my school district, everyone thinks that as superintendent, I make all the decisions. Only in my dreams—and nightmares! Here's our actual process: My management team makes recommendations to the school board, and the board makes decisions on all key aspects of our district budget, policy, strategic direction, and community engagement.

Some additional detail: Before my management team makes a recommendation to the board, the team has already run the bases and used good processes.

- We gathered all the INFORMATION on the issue at hand.
- We solicited REACTIONS to this issue.
- We brainstormed all the best OPTIONS, vetting this list of options by highlighting the pros and cons of each of the brainstormed options.
- Once these tasks have been completed, we can begin to discern which options have the greatest potential and which options have little team support because of the many cons uncovered.
- Our team narrows the list of remaining options to identify the best recommendation. We bring that idea forward to the board as our management team recommendation, and the board engages in further process to make DECISIONS.

I know a real estate agent, and in that world things operate differently. The agent collaborates with the client to sell or purchase a property. While the real estate agent would like to make all the decisions, it's the customer who's in control. It's their home and money at stake.

A reminder for everyone in the business of sales: If you want to increase your sales, simply make sure your client touches every base. Your sales will accelerate, along with your success average (your Leadership Batting Average), by simply getting your clients all the Information, Reactions, and Options, so they can make better, faster team Decisions.

I have another friend who owns several restaurants. A couple years ago, the friend came to me because one of the restaurants was declining in sales and revenue. The owner gathered staff. These team members wouldn't decide what would happen next with the restaurant, but the owner wanted their input and to inform them of the difficult news of the shortfall.

The restaurant owner made time for three separate meetings with restaurant staff:

- At the first meeting, the owner shared all the relevant updates and revenue information.
- At the second meeting, staff voiced their concerns, and the owner disclosed their concerns, including that on this trajectory the restaurant couldn't remain open.
- At the third meeting, staff offered their ideas and brainstormed options for the next version of a possible restaurant reset.

The restaurant staff didn't get to choose what happened next. They didn't even make final recommendations, which would be expected of a management team. But this example shows how even in small, closely held businesses, you can run the bases to get more information, solicit feedback, and explore ideas. Owners can support and elevate the voices of their employees while getting good direction for the future.

As you consider your own business, here are some additional dos and don'ts:

The board can avoid dipping into management issues by following this template ("The Governance Institute," 2018):

- Ensuring focus on the mission
- Setting direction and measurable goals

- Developing board-level (not operation) policies
- Ensuring systems and processes are in place and functioning well
- Monitoring progress and holding management accountable

Policy formulation. Boards formulate policy to give the organization direction. Policies are statements of intent that guide and constrain further decision making and action and limit subsequent choices. Policies provide a framework for the decision-making roles. ("The Governance Institute," 2018, p. 2)

Decision making. This is considered to be the most important role of governance, since much of what boards do eventually comes down to making choices. Decisions are based on policy. A board can choose to retain authority with respect to an issue related to one of its responsibilities or the board can delegate decision-making authority to management or the medical staff. ("The Governance Institute," 2018, p. 2)

Oversight. This is central to everything boards do. In fact, it is fundamental to governance core duties, roles, and responsibilities. Boards engage in oversight by monitoring decisions and actions to ensure they conform with policy and produce intended results. Management and the medical staff are accountable to the board for the decisions they make and the actions they undertake. Proper oversight ensures this accountability. ("The Governance Institute," 2018, p. 2)

IROD Chapter Review Questions	
I	What are your key takeaways from this chapter?
R	What reactions do you have to the information shared in this chapter?
O	How did this chapter's ideas offer ways to enhance your decision-making process?
D	What ideas from this chapter could you apply immediately to your team's decision-making?

For bonus video clips, go to **HomerunLeadership.com/Bonus**

CHAPTER 20

Where Homerun Leadership Matters Most

Coming together is a beginning, staying together is progress, and working together is success.

HENRY FORD

By this point, you no doubt can envision how Homerun Leadership Types and Team Decisions apply to the team that's always top of mind for you—perhaps the group that demands the most of your time and energy.

I now want to take a moment to help you think broadly about the why, where, and how of implementing this process.

Along the way, I'm going to ask a few straightforward questions I want you to reflect on.

The Why of Homerun Leadership

The day-in day-out focus of Homerun Leadership Types is reaching the best possible team decisions. Increasing your success rate! But there are important side benefits built into the system.

- **Homerun Leadership boosts DIVERSITY, EQUITY, AND INCLUSION.** As you put the IROD process to work, you're inviting everyone in the room to bring the best of their Leadership Type and contribute to the process. As you seek out Information, Reactions, and Options, you have a reason to solicit input from people outside the walls of your meeting room. Think about all the people impacted by your decisions. How will you include their voices in your decision making?

- **Homerun Leadership empowers LEADERSHIP, EMPLOYEE, AND VOLUNTEER ENGAGEMENT.** Little is more essential to an organization than regularly and sincerely reminding people that they matter. Proving it with actions! The mindset built into Homerun Leadership is that all people have value. Each person has unique gifts to offer. The openness of the process creates healthy environments where people willingly give heart and mind to the work you do together.

- **Homerun Leadership defuses CONFLICT.** If your team is in open warfare, you might need help from a system with conflict resolution as its primary goal. But a habit of running the Homerun Leadership Basepath provides constant opportunities for individuals and groups to productively discuss their differences and reach decisions together. It lowers the temperature of heated situations and eases the tensions of everyday team interactions.

Reflection Questions

What decision-making benefits do you anticipate for your team as you implement IROD Homerun Leadership methods?

What additional benefits do you see for using Homerun Leadership with your team?

The Where of Homerun Leadership

Life revolves around teams and teamwork!

We're all on many teams. Whenever you and one or more other people are responsible for making decisions together, you're a team. Merriam-Webster defines the word "team" as "people associated together in work or activity," and used as a verb, "team" is defined as "working together to achieve a common goal."

For example, here's just a sample of teams I'm on:

* School District leadership/management team
* School Board
* Family—the team of my wife and children
* My wife and I—our partnership
* Church Board—the team governance found in most nonprofits
* My pastor and I—a mutual coaching relationship

Take a minute to consider all the teams you participate in. It might help to picture your life in time segments—your days, weeks, months, and years—and all the people you interact with in a decision-making capacity.

Make this list as thorough as you can manage. Think about the multiple work teams you are a part of, the various family teams, the volunteer groups, and more. And for each—what are your key decision-making tasks?

More examples:

- If you're an HR Director, you're part of an Executive team, you might have staff reporting to you, and you have a boss. Each of those teams makes decisions. Where could you use help making effective team decisions? How will that enhance your leadership ability?
- If you're an organizational leader, you have an Executive team, community groups, a school board, and peer groups, all of which make decisions. Your ability to lead these groups into effective decision making directly affects your reputation, success, and effectiveness.
- Work leadership team—allocation of resources.
- Peer groups at work—choosing a theme for office event.
- Manager and assistant/employee—direction, presentations, projects.
- Business partnership—prioritizing partnership goals and objectives.
- Volunteer organization—fundraisers to use this year.
- Spouse—plans from the next minute to the rest of life.
- Siblings—who's in charge of the remote today?
- Parents and children—you might be the parent or the child or both— what movie should we go see tonight?
- Friend group—where are we going to go for dinner on Friday?
- Faith community—purpose and vision, including pathways to growth and impact.

You don't have to have a title or formal position as team leader to help move your team forward. In fact, the team member with the most knowledge about how to lead and move the team typically rises to the de facto team leader. Knowing about Homerun Leadership Types equips you to help your team move forward better and lead faster.

If you're the person with the position and power, you'll want to enlist all team members in taking a turn in leading Homerun Leadership decision-making meetings.

Reflection Questions: My Teams

What teams am I on?	How could each team benefit from IROD?

The How of Homerun Leadership

You can deploy Homerun Leadership with every team
    to make decisions
        and move forward
            in even the most complicated situations.

But WHEN can you introduce this powerful process? And HOW?

Consider these four IROD opportunities:

1. Run the Homerun Leadership Basepath for a small team decision. Providing a brief description before you start sets the stage for your trial run. There's nothing to lose!
2. Tackle a big decision. Some leaders jump right into complicated decisions with far-reaching consequences. They recognize the science behind IROD and realize the process is just what they need.
3. Address team stress. As I coach Homerun Leadership with new groups, I often start with an informal team stress test. It quickly points out the group's need for IROD, and the invitation to honest evaluation in itself paves the way for implementing the process.

Team Stress Test

I want you to think about your top team, that is, the group you lead or participate in that has the greatest impact. This might not be the team with the most decision-making power in the traditional sense. Think instead of which team has the potential to innovate and improve life and work for the most people.

In my school district, for example, our management team works together to devise creative solutions for complex and changing problems. They present their solutions to the District Board, which holds the power to vote yes or no. But the management team is the innovation center. We would get nowhere without the in-depth work of these leaders. So when I think "top team," it's often the management team over the Board.

Keep your own top team in mind as you answer this 10-question quiz. **After answering** TRUE or FALSE to each question, go back and count the number of times you answered TRUE.

	Circle TRUE or FALSE	
I dread going into my team meetings.	TRUE	FALSE
I am frequently frustrated during my team meetings.	TRUE	FALSE
Our meetings often run longer than scheduled.	TRUE	FALSE
Team members are reluctant to share thoughts and ideas.	TRUE	FALSE
Our team struggles to make decisions.	TRUE	FALSE
Our team discussions feel chaotic, lacking in organization or direction.	TRUE	FALSE
Our team lacks chemistry, connection, or trust.	TRUE	FALSE
Strong personalities dominate our team discussions.	TRUE	FALSE
Our team discussions often turn into arguments.	TRUE	FALSE
Our team meetings are a waste of time.	TRUE	FALSE
TOTAL "TRUE" ANSWERS		

How many times did you answer True? That's your score! And here's a scale for you to check your results:

Team Stress Scale

0	2	4	6	8	10
None	Minor	Moderate	Significant	High	Extreme

Team stress is normal. But that doesn't mean it's desirable. Among those 10 questions, none displays a quality that will help a team make decisions or advance its purposes. Each question indicates poor process.

If you find yourself at the high end of this continuum, the good news is the higher your score, the more progress you can make—relatively quickly—using Homerun Leadership.

So what about you? Let's take a minute and reflect on your team. Is your team causing you high levels of stress—and you are not sure why? Or is your team super successful—and operating with low levels of stress as you work through problems together?

Reflection Questions: My Team Stress

What causes stress in your top team?

How does Regular Leadership cause you stress?

What prevents you from using Homerun Leadership strategies with your teams?

How do you envision implementing Homerun Leadership with your team?

And here's yet another chance to try Homerun Leadership.

4: The Dread Ahead

"The Dread Ahead" is implementing IROD in whatever situation weighs most heavily on you right now. It's creating a specific framework for that anxiety-inducing situation.

Before you go into your team meeting, if you really want to satisfy the needs of all four Leadership Types, structure the meeting to answer the following questions. Remember your goal is to ensure all voices are heard as you touch all the bases to reach the best, fastest decision together.

Use these steps to adapt the language of the IROD Questions to your upcoming struggle:

What is your "dread-ahead" situation?

What is your goal in this situation?

What specific questions will help your team run the Homerun Basepath?

HOMERUN QUESTION	CLEAN-UP QUESTION
I	
R	
O	
D	

When you've gathered all the Information, Reactions, and Options, you'll resolve your dreaded issue by reaching the best Decision.

5: Daily Practice Running the Bases

As a reminder, if you're looking for a daily opportunity to consistently practice your Homerun Leadership base running skills, use the "What's for Dinner?" framework. After all, you need to choose something to eat every day, so why not build your family relationships and IROD performance at the same time? Each time you fail—and you will—you can start fresh again the next day, helping you smooth out the bumps in your process and relationships. Here's a blank framework for practice. If you need the full example with sample questions, feel free to use the complete "What's for Dinner?" framework earlier in the book.

Blank Homerun Framework					
I	INFORMATION question:				Anything else?
R	REACTIONS question:				Anything else?
O	Have we brainstormed all OPTIONS, listed pros and cons for each, and prioritized the list?				Anything else?
	Our Brainstormed OPTIONS	PROS	CONS	Reprioritized Options List	
	1.	1.	1.	1. 2.	
	2.	2.	2.	3.	
	3.	3.	3.		
D	Is the DECISION the will of the group?				Anything else?

	IROD Chapter Review Questions
I	What are your key takeaways from this chapter?
R	What reactions do you have to the information shared in this chapter?
O	How did this chapter's ideas offer ways to enhance your decision-making process?
D	What ideas from this chapter could you apply immediately to your team's decision-making?

For bonus video clips, go to **HomerunLeadership.com/Bonus**

CHAPTER 21

The Homerun Conclusion

It could be. It might be. It is! A home run!

HARRY CARAY—American Sportscaster

At the start of Homerun Leadership and Team Decisions, I explained why IROD is a critical tool. Some people collect cars or stamps. I collect Homeruns and team wins. For me, IROD is the most valuable, universal, one-size-fits-all tool in my toolkit. No matter what the problem or challenge I face with my many teams, IROD helps me fix it or improve it.

IROD helps me shift from Regular Leadership to Homerun Leadership. That's my dream for you:

Now that you know your Homerun Leadership Type…

Now that you can describe the qualities of the four Leadership Types on your team…

Now that you know the questions to ask to satisfy the needs of those four types,

All you need is one more thing: PRACTICE.

You just need practice problem solving and decision making with your team. Lots and lots of practice will help you to become the best Homerun Leader.

Let me close with a final story and a few last reminders.

The only thing better than hitting Homeruns is when the people you care about most start hitting Homeruns and increase their own success average (their Leadership Batting Average). As I recently drove my youngest daughter back to college, she said, "Dad, do you know I've been hitting homerun after homerun at college?"

Time in the car with my kids always seems to make them more free to open up about their lives. This day caught me off guard. While I've been working on my Homerun Leadership project for a long time, as a parent, it's tough to know exactly how much of what I do rubs off on my kids.

"Really?" I said. "Can you give me examples?"

"Sure," she said. "Well, my biggest hit was in my last class right before the big football weekend game between St. Thomas (my alma mater – Go Tommies!) and St. John's. My professor started class by telling us the assignments for the week, and we all noticed she had scheduled an 80-page reading assignment along with a 3-page paper over this super important weekend. Dad, you should have seen the students in my class. They reacted! "There's absolutely no way that assignment is getting done!" and a few "That's okay. I wasn't going to read it anyway."

I looked at the schedule and saw the assignment for the next class was just a 15-page reading. So I did what any Homerun student would. I asked the professor if there was a reason for the 80-page reading and essay over Tommy-Johnnie weekend instead of during the next week, when we'd have more free time. She said, "Oh! When is the Tommy-Johnnie game? I don't follow football so I didn't even think of that." The whole class yelled, "THIS WEEKEND!"

Once we explained that the big game was the same weekend as her big assignment, she was more than happy to push the reading back to make space. She wasn't out to get us. She simply didn't have all the information she needed when she scheduled assignments. By giving her a few more facts, we avoided having the weekend ruined with a huge homework assignment!"

My daughter shared that as class was dismissed, it was like the end of a baseball game where the team carries the player who just hit the game-winning homerun off the field. Everyone was giving her high-fives and saying, "Way to go! How did you manage to do that?!"

I couldn't have been more proud of my homegrown Homerun hitter!

EXTRA INNINGS: Complex Homeruns

Before ending this book, I want to alert you to a few curveballs. This next example is one of many situations that may be tougher to manage because it involves people that are frustrated or angry—a team in disarray, employees or children in conflict, complaints about you. I will have many more examples of 4 great questions to ask in these situations on my website. To get you started, I wanted to highlight one of the most common challenges for teams.

Run the Bases:
A Restorative plan for a Team

Teams that work together making frequent high-level, difficult decisions often need restorative conversations after situations get tense. This is especially true when teams face tight deadlines or are asked to make difficult decisions without full information or time for adequate discussion and process. When the team feels injured by these factors, a restorative conversation will help repair relationships. Here are four restorative questions to guide your conversation.

A RESTORATIVE PLAN FOR A TEAM Use these questions to guide a restorative conversation with your team.			
I	1st	Can we each share our perspectives on what happened?	Anything else?
R	2nd	Can we each share how we feel about what we have heard from one another?	Anything else?
O	3rd	Can we each share what we need?	Anything else?
D	4th	Can we each share what we can agree to as we move forward?	Anything else?

Here are a few last reminders:

◆ Don't let your greatest strength become your greatest weakness. Support all four Types on your teams.
◆ If you get stuck—and you will—move back to move forward. Go back and make sure you touch each base.
◆ Make the Homerun Basepath visible. Using a visual aid helps your team fully participate and engage. It supports better brainstorming.
◆ Don't go into your next meeting alone. Find a friend to co-facilitate. Misery loves company, and leading is hard work.

- Keep learning and growing your IROD skillset. HomerunLeadership. com provides support materials for you to keep growing into a Homerun Leader.
- Help your boss. One of the fastest ways up the chain of command is to help your boss, especially one who doesn't know IROD. Share the framework, this book, and the website. Help your whole team increase its success rate.
- Once your team reaches a Homerun decision or agreement, and you craft your communication plan to share with others, make sure you continue to follow the IROD framework as you share how and why the decision was made. Always share information first, then the reactions the team had or any anticipated concerns. Then share the options that were studied, along with the pros and cons that ultimately helped tip the scales in favor of this team decision. In large organizations, decisions may be affecting the lives of many others. By aligning your communication to IROD, you will help bring others along with you , and help followers better understand the complete decision-making process.

Thanks for staying engaged until the end. Team decision making is my passion, because I believe it's the most important team leader skill.

Our Homerun Leadership support team is available for your business, school, and church training events, as well as executive coaching. We've seen it's often helpful for new leaders to begin with an executive coaching experience, then introduce Homerun Leadership strategies to their team or into their organization. The leader who gets a head start can keep the momentum going within the organization as they support their various teams and boards.

Our Homerun support is available for you, too, via our HomerunLeadership. com website, where you can get help whenever you need it. We'll help you achieve HOMERUN SUCCESS!

Go hit and collect your own Homeruns, together with your team!

All the best,
Dave

	IROD Chapter Review Questions
I	What are your key takeaways from this book?
R	What reactions do you have to the information shared in this book?
O	How did this book's ideas offer ways to enhance your decision-making process?
D	What ideas from this book could you apply immediately to your team's decision-making?

For bonus video clips, go to **HomerunLeadership.com/Bonus**

About HomerunLeadership.com

You can find these resources and more at HomerunLeadership.com:

1. The Homerun Leadership book is designed to increase leadership performance. This is a great tool for team book studies and discussion.
2. The Self-Paced Video Course will help you run the bases. The course, accessible 24 hours a day, helps prepare you to lead your team.
3. The Digital Facilitation Package is a team facilitation toolkit providing digital tools to help you lead your next team meeting to get better, faster team decisions.
4. Gain access to Executive Coaching and Executive Team Coaching support.
5. Attend Dr. Dave Webb(inars)—Live Online Homerun Leadership Training Events.

About the Author

Dr. Dave Webb is a retired Superintendent of South St. Paul Public Schools. Dave previously served as a high school principal for Fridley Public Schools, and began his career as a Spanish teacher for the Stillwater Public Schools in Minnesota. Dave has also served as an Adjunct Faculty Member at Hamline University, the Dean of the Spanish Immersion Program for the Concordia Language Villages in Minnesota, and is currently the governing board president of his church in Shoreview, Minnesota.

Dr. Webb's passion for collaborative team decision-making grew out of his doctoral research in conflict management and shared decision-making. For decades, Dave's hallmark leadership style was defined by the principles of collaborative team decision-making, consensus building and inclusive team participation. His focus centers on helping individuals and organizations like businesses, schools and churches utilize the best collaborative team decision-making models.

In a variety of ways, Dr. Webb coaches both individuals and leadership teams in his simplified team science to move from point A to B. Dr. Webb provides easy-to-understand, memorable, repeatable processes that will help you and your team make great decisions and give you a framework applicable to ANY situation and EVERY meeting.

Notes

These authors are cited for their work in this book:

Bader, B. S. (2008). Great Boards: Distinguishing governance from management. *Bader an Associates Governance Consultants.* Maryland.

Conbere, J. (1996). *Mediation to Resolve Staff Conflicts.* MN: Stillwater.

Eisenstein, L. (2021, July 22). Governance vs management difference. BoardEffect. Retrieved February 27, 2022, from https://www.boardeffect.com/blog/difference-between-governance-management/.

Gossen, D. C. (1996). *Restitution: Restructuring school discipline.* New View Publications.

Hanson, M. P. (2005). *Clues to Achieving Consensus: A Leader's Guide to Navigating Collaborative Problem Solving.* R&L Education.

Karten, N. (2012, October 17). *How team norms can boost team effectiveness.* Techwell. Retrieved March 23, 2022, from https://www.techwell.com/2012/10/how-team-norms-can-boost-team-effectiveness/.

School Reform Initiative. (2017, March 30). *Compass Points: North, South, East, and West - An Exercise in Understanding Preferences in Group Work*. Retrieved January 3, 2022, from https://www.schoolreforminitiative.org/download/compass-points-north-south-east-and-west-an-exercise-in-understanding-preferences-in-group-work/.

Senge, P. (1990). *The Fifth Discipline: The Art and Practice of the Learning Organization*. New York, NY: Doubleday.

Spencer, L. J. (1989). *Winning Through Participation*. Kendall/Hunt Publishing Company.

Stanfield, R. B. (1997). *The Art of Focused Conversation: 100 Ways to Access Group Wisdom in the Workplace*. Ontario, Canada: The Canadian Institute of Cultural Affairs.

Technology of Participation. (n.d.). *Training Modules*. Retrieved January 3, 2022, from https://www.top-training.net/w/.

The Governance Institute. (2018). *The Distinction between Management and Governance (2nd Edition)*. Elements of Governance Series. San Diego, CA.

Notes II

The following authors were each cited in my dissertation, "The Invisible Path to Shared Decision-making" that I published in 2001. While many of these were not specifically mentioned or used directly in this book, I believed that it is important to give them credit for their work, as their writings have influenced my team decision-making skills over the past 20 years.

Argyris, C., & Schon, D. (1996). *Organizational Learning II: Theory, Method and Practice Reading.* Boston, MA: Addison Wesley.

Biklen, S. K., & Bogden, R. C. (1982). *Qualitative Research for Education: An Introduction to Theory and Methods.* Needham Height. MA: Allyn & Bacon.

Blumer, H. (1969). *Symbolic Interactionism* (Vol. 50). Englewood Cliffs, NJ: Prentice-Hall.

Bolman, L., & Deal, T. (1997). *Reframing Organizations.* San Francisco, CA: Jossey-Bass Publishers.

Burns, J.M. (1978). *Leadership.* New York, NY: Harper & Row.

Carroll, J. M. (1990). *The Copernican Plan: Restructuring the American High School. The Phi Delta Kappan, 71*(5), 358-365.

Carroll, J. M. (1994). *Organizing Time to Support Learning. The School Administrator, 57*(3), 26–33.

Charon, J. (1979). *Symbolic Interactionism: an introduction, an interpretation, an integration.* Upper Saddle River, New Jersey: Simon & Schuster.

Cushman, K. (1995). "Using Time Well: Schedules in Essential Schools." *Horace, 12*(2), 1-8.

Drath, W. H., & Palus, C. J. (1994). "Making Common Sense: Leadership as Meaning-making in a Community of Practice." Greensboro, NC: Center for Creative Leadership.

Evans, D. L. (1995). Some reflections on doing the principalship. *National Association of Secondary School Principals Bulletin, 79*(567), 4-15.

Fullan, M. (1991). *The New Meaning of Educational Change.* New York, NY: Teachers College Press.

Fullan, M. (1997). *The Challenge of School Change: A Collection of Articles.* Arlington Heights, IL: IRI/Skylight Training and Publishing, Inc.

Hottenstein, D. (1998). *Intensive Scheduling: Restructuring America's Secondary Schools Through Time Management.* Thousand Oaks, CA: Corwin Press.

Kaner, S. (1996). *Facilitator's Guide to Participatory Decision-making.* Montpelier, Vermont: Capital City Press.

Lincoln, B. (1989). *Discourse and the Construction of Society.* New York, New York: Oxford University Press.

Mottaz, C. A. (1999). *Alternative Education in Minnesota: How do we know it works?*(Order No. 9953945). Available from ProQuest Dissertations & Theses Global. (304569836).

National Association of Secondary School Principals. (1996). "Breaking Ranks: Changing an American Institution." Reston, VA: National Association of Secondary School Principals.

National Commission on Excellence in Education. (1983). *A Nation at Risk.* Washington, DC: U.S. Government Printing Office.

Sagor, R. (1992). "Three Principals Who Make a Difference." Educational Leadership 49 (5), 13-18.

Senge, P. (1990). *The Fifth Discipline: The Art and Practice of the Learning Organization.* New York, NY: Doubleday.

Smyth, J. (1989). *Critical Perspectives on Educational Leadership.* New York, NY: The Falmer Press.

Spencer, L. J. (1989). *Winning Through Participation.* Dubuque, Iowa: Kendall/Hunt Publishing Company.

Stanfield, R. B. (1997). *The Art of Focused Conversation: 100 Ways to Access Group Wisdom in the Workplace.* Ontario, Canada: The Canadian Institute of Cultural Affairs.

Ury, W. (1991). *Getting Past No: Negotiating with Difficult People.* New York, NY: Bantam Books.

Wagner, T. (2001). "Leadership for Learning: An Action Theory of School Change." *Phi Delta Kappan, 82*(5), 378-383.

Webb, D. (2001). *The invisible path to shared decision-making: A comparative case study of two schools attempts to overcome barriers to change.* St. Paul, MN: University of St. Thomas.

Whitaker, T. (2000). *Motivating and Inspiring Teachers: The Educational Leader's Guide for Building Staff Morale.* Larchmont, NY: Eye on Education.

Made in the USA
Monee, IL
02 February 2024

52811845R00094